A Reader's Guide to
John Barth

A Reader's Guide to *John Barth*

Zack Bowen

Greenwood Press
Westport, Connecticut • London

813.54
B284
c.1

Library of Congress Cataloging-in-Publication Data

Bowen, Zack R.
    A reader's guide to John Barth / Zack Bowen.
      p.   cm.
    Includes bibliographical references and index.
    ISBN 0-313-27978-0 (alk. paper)
    1. Barth, John—Criticism and interpretation.   I. Title.
PS3552.A75Z56   1994
813'.54—dc20   93-10378

British Library Cataloguing in Publication Data is available.

Copyright © 1994 by Zack Bowen

All rights reserved. No portion of this book may be reproduced, by any process or technique, without the express written consent of the publisher.

Library of Congress Catalog Card Number: 93-10378
ISBN: 0-313-27978-0

First published in 1994

Greenwood Press, 88 Post Road West, Westport, CT 06881
An imprint of Greenwood Publishing Group, Inc.

Printed in the United States of America

The paper used in this book complies with the Permanent Paper Standard issued by the National Information Standards Organization (Z39.48-1984).

10 9 8 7 6 5 4 3 2 1

Copyright Acknowledgments

The author and publisher gratefully acknowledge permission to reproduce the following copyrighted material:

John Barth, *Chimera*. Copyright © 1972 by John Barth. Reprinted by permission of Random House, Inc.

John Barth, *The Floating Opera*. Copyright © 1976 by John Barth. Reprinted by permission of Doubleday, a Division of Bantam, Doubleday, & Dell Publishing Group, Inc.

John Barth, *Giles Goat-Boy*. Copyright © 1987 by John Barth. Reprinted by permission of Doubleday, a Division of Bantam, Doubleday, & Dell Publishing Group, Inc.

John Barth, *The Last Voyage of Somebody the Sailor*. Copyright © 1991 by John Barth. Reprinted by permission of Little, Brown and Company.

For Lindsey

Contents

Acknowledgments		ix
Introduction		xi
Abbreviations, First Editions, and Editions Used		xv
1.	Barth's Transient Opera: *The Floating Opera*	1
2.	Mythoscriptotherapy: *The End of the Road* and the Novel of Ideas	13
3.	The New *Marylandiad*: Barth as Poet Laureate in *The Sot-Weed Factor*	21
4.	The Revised New Syllabus: *Giles Goat-Boy*	35
5.	Funhouse Reflexes: *Lost in the Funhouse*	51
6.	Narrators and Heroes in *Chimera*	67
7.	History, Sex, and Art in John Barth's *LETTERS*	81
8.	*Sabbatical*: Conception Concepts in the Chesapeake Womb-World	99
9.	Chiasmus in the Womb-World: Doubling in *The Tidewater Tales*	109

10.	Replenishment and Reproduction: *The Last Voyage of Somebody the Sailor*	119

Appendix 1: Selected List of Recurrent Themes, Patterns, and Techniques — 131

Appendix 2: Biographical Note on John Barth — 137

Selected Bibliography — 139

Index — 147

Acknowledgments

This book was conceived more than twenty years ago, when I began to teach Barth in classes at the State University of New York at Binghamton. I was deep into James Joyce scholarship when, like so many others, I began to read and respond to Barth's omnivorous intellect, technical brilliance, and satiric outlook on life. For me Barth was the most daring, funny man I had read since Joyce, and the best part about his work was that, as with Joyce, there was so much to get excited about—to explain and discuss with classes—that teaching him was unadulterated pleasure. I first met Barth when he came to SUNY Binghamton for a reading, and my continuing thought during the hour or two I was privileged to speak to him personally was that, unlike some others I knew, I had never had the opportunity to talk to Joyce, and that now, thank the Dean, I was given the chance at last to be in the presence of greatness. I naively supposed I could perhaps be a Stuart Gilbert to Barth's Joyce.

However, the late 1960s and early 1970s saw an avalanche of Barth dissertations, then essays, eventually followed by books. I was heavily committed to ongoing Joyce projects, but had the luxury of exceptionally fine graduate research-assistant-colleagues who began to collect Barth scholarship for me. I am especially indebted to Marguerite Harkness, Barbara DiBernard, Ted Billy, and Paul Butera for their early help. Barth kept writing complicated epic tomes that required extensive reflection, and critics continued to publish the ideas I would have liked to have written, while I devoted my research time principally to Irish literature. With a current sabbatical and the help of a first-rate assistant, Adam Price, I am able at last to capitalize on the entire body of Barth scholarship in a commentary on all of Barth's ten novels, tracing the development of issues and techniques that run through his works. Finally, I am deeply indebted to Bartheans John Balaban, Joseph Weixlmann, and Susan Strehl for their time-consuming, informed reading of my manuscript, and to Lindsey Tucker, my Ultimate Editor, for curbing my excesses.

Introduction

John Barth's rich, complex novels offer so many opportunities for discussion, explication, and critical speculation that the reader scarcely knows where to begin. An intelligent class of informed students who love literature and welcome the challenge presented by difficult works can make teaching Barth a delight. Surprisingly, after ten volumes of fiction spanning forty-five years of steady production, his books remain as much a part of the curriculum as they ever were, his ideas as intriguing and controversial, his comedy and eroticism as clever and Rabelaisian. While in recent books the number of orgasms per chapter may even have increased along with Barth's variations on his own themes, he is still an exceptionally funny intellectual writer whose sense of humor is as appealing as his puzzles can be baffling.

His works, alternating among ludicrousness, deadly seriousness, and intense realism, are principally novels of ideas. His art itself is, in a way, on critical/philosophical trial with every work. So many alternatives, both to composition and meaning, are explored that the books become less artistic artifacts than propositions pursued to that point of absurdity which is also the perimeter of truth. Barth transforms the practice of reflexive literary criticism into philosophical speculation even as he produces the works in which his points are exemplified. That enormous self-absorption is reflected in all his work is recognized by critics pro and con, but the issue is debated most hotly in Barth's own fiction, and in particular in his theoretical centerpiece, *Lost in the Funhouse*.

While Barth gets the jump on the critics by discussing—either directly or indirectly—in each work most of the critical points that the fiction itself raises, he also explores the issues of his craft in a series of published interviews and essays, and in *The Friday Book*, a collection culled principally from talks he gave at various colleges and professional meetings. His most prominent ideas are represented in two landmark essays, "The Literature of Exhaustion" and "The Literature of Replenishment," which have nearly eclipsed his fiction in terms of their impact on contemporary literary criticism. While these documents provide a rationale for writing works informed by literary tradition, they also touch on the existential downside of Barth's philosophy. Grossly oversimplified, his essential message is that all the stories, tales, and yarns have been used up—that the ur-tales have already been told—but that the modern author can make an old statement new by regenerating the narrative process itself. In Barth's words, "Virtuosity is a virtue, and . . . what artists feel about the state of the world and the state of their art is less important than what they do with that feeling."[1] Barth's insistence on novelty and technical virtuosity of presentation calls for innovative parody: "Artistic conventions are liable to be retired, subverted, transcended, transformed, or even deployed against themselves to generate new and lively work."[2] Barth practices what he preaches, and his fiction is to a great extent the ingenious embodiment of those ideas.

This book was written for intelligent first readers of Barth. It is not intended as a substitute for reading, but as enhancement for those who have already read the individual works with some care. Thus my individual readings do not restate the obvious or rehash plots, but try to build a perspective based on informed close readings of the texts. While taking cognizance of the major published Barth criticism, each chapter offers a new interpretation of one of Barth's fictional works, and may for the most part be read separate from the others. The book encompasses all of Barth's major fiction, primarily explicating rather than seeking to frame any work in a single contemporary critical theory. Where theoretical issues are raised, they are explained in general terms rather than in the vernacular of the individual theory, even though further explanation of and sources for the theory itself may be found in footnotes. Where discussion of patterns or images from other Barth books illuminates the text discussed, I have not refrained from making such comparisons—especially in the light of Barth's constant allusions to his previous and even forthcoming works—in an attempt to identify the continuity of Barth's recurring ideas.

Barth's works are so pregnant with critical possibilities that while they demand full critical treatment, they also offer such a variety that no book can pretend to provide a definitive answer for any text. Instead, this study makes full use of those previous interpretations that seem to make the most sense, and at the same time tries to offer a new and unique perspective on each novel. So intertwined are Barth's repetitive motifs, themes, and characters in his own fiction that I have offered a separate appendix pointing to a selection of such recurrent patterns.

Over the last four decades Barth has attracted the attention of a number of exceptionally perceptive critics, and this book has profited by their insights. It seems to me that Barth criticism has become increasingly sophisticated as scholars have had more time to digest and assemble the variegated strands of his fiction. Jac Tharpe wrote the first full-length study of Barth in 1976,[3] and, while he covers only Barth's early works through *Chimera*, many of Tharpe's insights remain valuable today. Likewise, much of the Barth criticism that followed David Morrell's ground-breaking *John Barth: An Introduction*—which detailed material on Barth's sources, personal history, and process of composition—owes Morrell a debt of gratitude.[4]

The eighties elaborated and expanded the influence of the previous decade's best scholarship, beginning with Joseph Waldmeir's edition of collected essays.[5] Three years later, Charles Harris revised some of his earlier seminal works for inclusion in his *Passionate Virtuosity*, which developed through a principally historical-philosophical perspective the way in which Barth attempts to resolve the problems about reality and how a writer's language tries to deal with or recreate it.[6]

E. P. Walkiewicz's book on Barth is the first to attempt a popular summary and critical reading of Barth works (through *Tidewater Tales*) for a larger nonscholarly Barth audience.[7] Walkiewicz was followed by Heide Ziegler's sensitive readings of Barth works through *Sabbatical*. Ziegler's interpretations are structured on Barth's "twinning" pairs of novels, in which Barth "exhausts" a literary/philosophical tradition in the first and "replenishes" it in the second.[8] The final book in the readers' guide genre is Stan Fogel and Gordon Slethaug's *Understanding John Barth*.[9]

Max Schulz's work, especially on Barth's self-reflexive approach to literary history, mythic background, modern philosophy, and contemporary affairs, represents some of the most informed and intelligent criticism written on Barth. His book *The Muses of John Barth* deals principally with *Lost in the Funhouse* and succeeding works through *Tidewater Tales*.[10]

The most recent volume of criticism on Barth to date is Patricia Tobin's *John Barth and the Anxiety of Continuance*, a study of Barth's works through the lens of Harold Bloom's anxiety of influence theory.[11] Bloom's idea is so obviously applicable to Barth that it is a mystery why no one has made the connection before. Tobin's perceptive analysis was long overdue.

Because so much Barth criticism has appeared in essay form, the proliferation of articles, theses, and dissertations on Barth resembles the federal deficit. Unlike the deficit, however, the scholarship has slowed in recent years, even as the major studies in book form have appeared. Except for

Waldmeir's essay collection, all the books mentioned above contain fairly extensive bibliographies, and many of the most perceptive critical points have been restated so often as to fall into the public domain. While I have included a bibliography of selected criticism in this book, readers needing still further clarification of Barth's later works might be well advised to look at the bibliographies of the more recently published criticism mentioned above. Two separate book-length bibliographies of Barth criticism through 1975 are available, but Joseph Weixlmann's version is by far the better annotated, and more complete and authoritative. The seventeen years of criticism since Weixlmann cry out for a new, comprehensive bibliography.[12] Still, the riches buried in Barth's fiction have only begun to be mined, and I hope that what new perspectives are contained in the following chapters may yet add something to our understanding of this complicated, gifted writer.

NOTES

1. John Barth, introduction to "The Literature of Exhaustion," in *The Friday Book: Essays and Other Nonfiction* (New York: Perigee Books/Putnam, 1984), p. 64.

2. John Barth, "The Literature of Replenishment," in *The Friday Book*, p. 205.

3. Jac Tharpe, *John Barth: The Comic Sublimity of Paradox* (Carbondale: Southern Illinois University Press, 1974).

4. David Morrell, *John Barth: An Introduction* (University Park: Pennsylvania State University Press, 1976).

5. Joseph J. Waldmeir, ed., *Critical Essays on John Barth* (Boston: G. K. Hall, 1980).

6. Charles B. Harris, *Passionate Virtuosity: The Fiction of John Barth* (Urbana: University of Illinois Press, 1983).

7. E. P. Walkiewicz, *John Barth* (Boston: Twayne, 1986).

8. Heide Ziegler, *John Barth* (London: Methuen, 1987).

9. Stan Fogel and Gordon Slethaug, *Understanding John Barth* (Columbia: University of South Carolina Press, 1990).

10. Max Schulz, *The Muses of John Barth: Tradition and Metafiction from "Lost in the Funhouse" to "The Tidewater Tales"* (Baltimore: Johns Hopkins University Press, 1990). Also, see bibliography for additional articles.

11. Patricia Tobin, *John Barth and the Anxiety of Continuance* (Philadelphia: University of Pennsylvania Press, 1992).

12. For a more recent, if attenuated, descriptive Barth bibliography, see Joseph Weixlmann's "John Barth," in *American Novelists,* Contemporary Authors: Bibliographical Series 1, ed. James J. Martine (Detroit: Gale, 1986), pp. 43–81.

Abbreviations, First Editions, and Editions Used

First editions (in parentheses) precede editions used.

C   *Chimera* (Random House, 1972). First edition used.
ER *The End of the Road* (Doubleday, 1958), Bantam, 1972.
FO *The Floating Opera* (Appleton-Century-Crofts, 1956), Bantam, 1976.
FB *The Friday Book: Essays and Other Nonfiction* (G. P. Putnam's Sons, 1984). First edition used.
G   *Giles Goat-Boy or, The Revised New Syllabus* (Doubleday, 1966), Anchor/Doubleday, 1987.
LV *The Last Voyage of Somebody the Sailor* (Little, Brown, 1991). First edition used.
L   *LETTERS* (G. P. Putnam's Sons, 1979). First edition used.
F   *Lost in the Funhouse: Fiction for Print, Tape, Live Voice* (Doubleday, 1968), Anchor/Doubleday, 1988.
S   *Sabbatical* (G. P. Putnam's, 1982). First edition used.
SWF *The Sot-Weed Factor* (Bantam, 1969). First edition used.
TWT *The Tidewater Tales* (Fawcett Columbine, 1987). First edition used.

1

Barth's Transient Opera: *The Floating Opera*

Opera is a transient, hybrid art calling for the suspension of the audience's sense of reality while the dialogue of drama, itself an imitation of reality, becomes the lyrics of an extended work of music. The music adds its own conventions of overture, repetition, and multiple-part singing, calling on its audience to believe that two or more characters simultaneously express identical ideas in unison or in harmony. Opera thus demands a suspension of credulity and an acceptance of form that few other artistic genres dictate. Float the whole performance on a barge drifting past an audience fixed in one observation point, as Todd Andrews's image demands, and the result is a fragmented knowledge of the opera's activities, chronology of events, or characters' motivations, coupled with a lack of hope for any comprehensive audience understanding.

Further complicating the situation is the conductor/narrator's own lack of understanding. While flawed narrators have been a part of English literature at least since Chaucer's time, the technique became identified with the modern literary experimentation of Ford Maddox Ford. *The Floating Opera* shares several characteristics with Ford's *The Good Soldier*: bad hearts, hopeless adulterous love triangles leading to suicides, and especially a confused first-person narrator who finds himself good at business though unconcerned with profit, and who writes down his history in a muddled effort to understand the meaning of his life. Dowell, Ford's protagonist, appeals to his audience for help in deciphering the meaning of the chaos around him, while Todd writes his journal in order to gain a private, personal perspective on his own problem as an aspect of his father's suicide. If he could understand or justify his father's action, he might be able to understand his own suicidal drive and/or his reason for not blowing up himself, his daughter, and most of the town. Whether or not the journal improves his insight into himself is open to question.

His present narrative, typical of Barth's books, is begun *in medias res*, and derives from his journal. It concerns principally the climactic events of June 23 or 24, 1937, which occurred seventeen years before Todd purportedly rewrote them for publication as a novel in 1954.[1] During the intervening years Todd has managed to provide himself with a hindsight philosophical rationale for his actions, but it is not certain that the wider general audience of the book is supposed to agree with either his premises or his motivations. On the contrary, Todd's mental predisposition is so problematical as to be almost ludicrous or burlesqued, despite its seeming insistence on existential logic.

The novel resembles *Tristram Shandy* in its beginning self-consciousness, when it openly addresses its readers about the difficulties of its own composition. Beginning in the middle, the book, again like *Shandy*, emphasizes time frames and periods, rightly claiming that events of Andrews's life that precede the climax are necessary to an understanding of his thinking on the day he intends to commit suicide. Thus Todd writes his book with two predominant if subliminal purposes: to explain himself as mentally recapitulating his father's supposed reasons for taking his own life, and at the same time to detail the tortured existential logic that propelled both father and son to ultimate questions and their common putative answers in the form of suicide.

The suspense of the novel stems from the question of what happened on the big June day seventeen years before, and why and how the contemplated suicide did *not* take place, since we already know Todd survived. The primary question is the perennial existential one, "To be or not to be," coupled with its logical extension, "Why *be* at all?", and its contemporary converse, "Why not?" The issue was particularly rife during the postwar existential movement, with Sartre's and Camus's ultimate answers differing with each other and with themselves over a period of time. The early existential dilemma involved freedom of choice versus an inherent indifference to the obligation to make any choice at all. To Sartre the question extended to whether or not to join the opposition to the forces of oppression: to absent oneself and leave the world to its own idiotic devices, or to take up arms against a sea of evils and, by opposing, end them, an idea of personal versus social obligation renewed in *The Floating Opera*.

The dilemma is reflected in the metaphoric structure of the novel: If life resembles a floating show, complete with masks and characters who meaninglessly act out roles, what use is there in understanding what it is all about? Why even make an attempt? The question of hopelessness raises the analogous question of why Todd should bother to write about it. The floating opera image acts as a reflexive metaphor of its own creation, and continues as the principal artistic conundrum of most of the works discussed in this volume. Todd discusses the creative rationale that ties not only this but Barth's ensuing books into his grand scheme:

> It always seemed a fine idea to me to build a showboat with just one big flat open deck on it, and to keep a play going continuously. The boat wouldn't be moored, but would drift up and down the river on the tide, and the audience would sit along both banks. They would catch whatever part of the plot happened to unfold as the boat floated past, and then they'd have to wait until the tide ran back again to catch another snatch of it, if they still happened to be sitting there. To fill in the gaps they'd just have to use their imaginations, or ask more attentive neighbors or hear the word passed along from upriver or downriver. Most times they wouldn't understand what was going on at all, or they'd think they knew, when actually they didn't. Lots of times they'd be able to see the actors, but not hear them. I needn't explain that that's how much of life works: our friends float past; we become involved with them; they float on, and we must rely on hearsay or lose track of them completely; they float back again, and we either renew our friendship—catch up to date—or find that they and we don't comprehend each other any more. And that's how this book will work, I'm sure. It's a floating opera, friend, fraught with curiosities, melodrama, spectacle, instruction, and entertainment. But it floats willy-nilly on the tide of my vagrant prose: you'll catch sight of it, lose it, spy it again; and it may require the best efforts of your attention and imagination—together with some patience, if you're an average fellow—to keep track of the plot as it sails in and out of view. (*FO* 7)

The elaborate metaphor itself, with its affinity to the images on the wall of Plato's Cave, testifies to the artifice and craftsmanship required to build such a fictive vessel, even as the image denigrates the role of fiction as the ideal mirror of reality. The vagrant sperm cell, water message, and amphorae of *Funhouse*, as well as the voyaging turd in *LETTERS* and the canister in *Tidewater*, are all variations on this theme of floating creative reflexivity. This chapter will elaborate on the ways in which the title barge of *The Floating Opera* becomes a sort of artistic flagship in Barth's Chesapeake fleet of concerns about the creative process.

During the days leading to his projected suicide, Todd is regularly involved in the second of two attempts to build floating crafts. The first, begun by a child who possessed only desire and imagination, lacked the craftsmanship and art necessary to be brought to successful completion, and the second, begun with deliberateness and care, is a work in progress, the nautical metaphor for that section of Todd's *Inquiry* that is to become the current book. Andrews's boat/book has its analogue in the *Thespian*, the registered name of the vessel with the trade name *Adam's Original & Unparalleled Floating Opera*. The *Opera* was built by one of Todd's several surrogates, Captain Adam, whose meticulous care and forethought in the ship's construction mirror Todd's own conduct of his life and boat building.

At least one major Barth critic posits his entire interpretation of the novel's meaning on Todd's being secure in his knowledge of the *Floating Opera*'s soundness: Andrews *knew* the boat would never have blown up, since care would have been taken to avoid such an instance occurring—an opinion apparently voiced by Barth himself in an interview.[2] This view stems from what Todd learned about the safety of the boat from Captain Adam during Todd and Jeannine's afternoon tour, when Andrews conceived the plan to destroy himself and the audience during the evening performance. If Todd knew that the suicide attempt would be at best a harmless and irrelevant formality without the possibility of fatal success, why bother to turn on the gas at all? After the show was safely over, he could have jumped in the river, but declined to make the effort on the ground that killing himself wasn't worth the bother. Certainly if he had stepped off the dock into the water, the chances of his being involuntarily rescued by anyone in the departing crowd were as great as the assumed safety of the boat's ventilation system. Why should he suppose that jumping had a greater chance of success than blowing up the boat? Todd's rationalized existentialism is indeed as nutty as Dowell's social imbecility.

Ford critics often see Dowell's ineffectuality as that of an innocent caught in an Edwardian moral morass, and blame the Ashburnham tragedy on the decadence of the entire society. There is much in Todd's history to explain away his own actions on similar grounds. According to Richard Schickel, Todd's grand rationalization of his suicidal existential philosophy is born of "five occasions on which he felt deep emotion,"[3] each a further realization that his emotions are intertwined with his actions and must be combatted with all the indifference his rationality can command.

His encounter with the German soldier in the foxhole—when Todd learns fear—is a primary instance of what Barth critics variously call his emotional climaxes or stages of psychological development. These scenes bear a strong resemblance to Joycean epiphanies. After befriending his would-be enemy to the point of total communion, Todd, afraid the next morning that the German might revert to something other than soul-mate, runs the German through with a bayonet. It is indeed a grisly scar on Todd's psyche.

At age seventeen Andrews discovers mirth—the ludicrousness of his all-consuming copulative aspirations—when he sees a mirrored image of himself in coitus with his first lover. What he learns is the ridiculousness of his own passion. While this incident chronologically occurs first, it is presented later in the text to keep the evolution of his reactive development uniform.

Todd's discovery of his father's body hanging by his belt with eyes bulging, but his clothes neat and orderly, introduces frustration into Todd's emotional catalogue, and the rest of his life is spent in trying to explain his father's reasons and to assess his own involvement in the death. Todd's reaction takes the forms of his *Inquiry* and his imitation of his father's desperate act.

Critics are split over which two emotional scenes complete the five needed to complement Todd's five *Inquiry* conclusions. Schickel first singles out Todd's "surprise when Jane . . . [creeps] into his bed one afternoon, uninvited but not unwelcome,"[4] and second, her later remark on Todd's clubbed fingers, introducing impotence, futility, and despair to his emotional catalogue.[5] Other critics recognize Jane's remark as an emotional turning point in Todd's decision to commit suicide, but also see concern as the major factor in Todd's saving Jeannine along with the other 700 townsfolk on *The Floating Opera* in the first published edition of the book, and Haecker's life in the restored original version of the text.[6]

The problem with the emotional-moments theory is that no one seems to want to admit the all-important scene with the army doctor, when Todd is told that he has an incurable, possibly fatal circulatory illness. While there is nothing in the way of an emotional outburst here, the information—imparted with cold matter-of-factness by the doctor—is the major factor influencing all Todd's subsequent feelings of impermanence. If learning that there is a good chance of imminent death doesn't shake your psyche, occasional impotence certainly shouldn't. Many of Todd's other activities may be laid to other causes, but his more expensive daily payment of overnight rent is both precaution against a possible overcharge when he does die, and a daily graphic reminder of the threat of mortality hanging over his head. He avoids any effort to verify the diagnosis, preferring to live as if it were true. Surely this must give rise to some of his offbeat mental processes.

For example, Todd's penchant for list-making—for tediously rehearsing and rerehearsing the stages of his own intellectual debate—adds an attitude of zaniness to his attempt to apply logical sophistry to human behavior and events. His list of his five stages of consciousness and his list of potential outcomes of the Harrison *ménage à trois* (qualified by their probability of materializing) both presage his final systematic sophistry about life and death:

I. Nothing has intrinsic value.
II. The reasons for which people attribute value to things are always ultimately irrational.

III. There is, therefore, no ultimate "reason" for valuing anything . . . including life . . .
IV. Living is action. There's no final reason for action.
V. There's no final reason for living . . . (or for suicide). (*FO* 218, 223, 245)

The final parenthesis, to the effect that suicide is as futile and hence valueless and irrational as continuing to live, provides the ultimate logical rationalization for Todd's behavior, the end of at least this discursive detour on his extended philosophical inquiry. It is not, however, the end of the book, which concludes with his going "to bed in enormous soothing solitude, and . . . [sleeping] fairly well despite the absurd thunderstorm that soon afterwards broke all around" (*FO* 247). The conclusion suggests that the irrational and the absurd have a special and important place in the cosmos, whether or not they are part of Todd's plan.

The order that Todd tries to bring to life is nothing less than an attempt to control the chaos of the cosmos insofar as it affects himself and his actions. At the end, before falling off to sleep, Todd revises his bequest of philosophical truisms for his dead father. Barth draws attention to the absurdity of Todd's revisions by inviting comparison with its counterpart in Harrison Mack Sr.'s oft revised seventeen-draft will, which constitutes a major portion of the book's legal/monetary comic subplot. Todd's success as a lawyer is predicated on his knowledge of irrationality, on his detached understanding of the absurd, which is made all the more ridiculous by its own crazy logic. The elder Mack's estate consists of money, property, pickles, and his personal fecal legacy. The excrement that Mack held so sacred is the ultimate factor in deciding who gets the estate. Todd's father, in heavy debt, leaves for his son just as inexplicable a legacy of problems regarding his reasons for suicide. No critic questions old Mack's insanity, even when he meticulously keeps in chronological order the repeated versions of his will. However, the courts, in their twisted logic, strive to maintain the precise moment he went berserk, on one hand, and, on the other, whether the turds' repositors completely fulfilled the terms of his idiotic legacy. Eventually, through the appellate process, the entire legal structure of the State, up to the Supreme Court of Appeals, is involved in Mack's nonsense. Because Todd is not emotionally involved in the substance of the case (pun intended), he can manipulate and order its absurdity to his own purpose, delaying the trial until a favorable group of judges sit to hear it. When the gardener exhibits the only trace of common sense in the case by suggesting that Mack's increasingly odoriferous fecal matter be put to use as garden fertilizer, he commits the very offense that will ultimately result in a reversal of the lower court's decision. The legal victory represents a triumph of absurd logic, one that only Todd, the cynic who cannot be cynical about his own absurd logic, is able to bring about.

The *Morton v. Butler* case represents another variation on the absurdity of the law when an accident causes a three-year litigation and an arena for local political rivalry. In the absurdity of legal entanglements that ensued, one of the litigants would have been forced to sue his own son in order to win his case against his opponent. Todd's involvement as Butler's defense lawyer stems from Andrews's totemization of Morton, whose Famous Tomatoes made him the richest man in town. At least one of the contributory factors to Todd's father's suicide was bad investments, which led the elder Andrews to the brink of bankruptcy. His only bequest to Todd was $5,000, which Todd gratuitously gives to the person who needs it least, the rich Colonel Henry W. Morton, thus rendering absurd Andrews Sr.'s reason for death. Morton's reaction to this undeserved and totally incongruous gift is to try to return it, then to try to compensate for it, and then to try to befriend Todd, and finally to despise him for both Todd's indiscretion with Morton's wife and Todd's aloofness regarding money. In a way Todd's disposition of his legacy makes about as much sense as old Mack's, and Morton's putative sharing of his wife at his party is a rough analogy to the absurdity of the triangle among Jane, young Mack, and Todd.

This brings us to the irrational nature of the *ménage à trois* that has caused Todd so much subliminal damage as well as pleasure over the years. The Macks, by a twist of Bohemian existentialist logic, seek at the same time to prove their love for each other by engaging in adultery. The relationship between Mack Jr. and Andrews has all of the classical elements of latent homosexuality in their sharing each other by sharing a woman. The Macks' premises for planned adultery are on the surface roughly analogous to Todd's desire for existential freedom. The Macks will liberate themselves by consciously giving Jane, and thus both, the freedom to choose among lovers denied by the marital institution. The Macks' cutesy rationalizations supply the domestic equivalent of Todd's skewed profundities about the meaning of existence. Ultimately all are victimized by guilt, jealousy, and, finally, indifference—emotion, passion, and erection sickly'd o'er by the pale cast of thought.

Like the activities of both serious and comic subplots, all of the characters with whom Todd associates come to inform his ruminations and actions. The most prominent are Osborn and Haecker, respectively the pro-lifer who enjoys existence by railing against it, and the eventual suicide whose conscious acceptance of his life belies a subliminal abhorrence of its condition. Along with Todd, they are Explorers' Club members, whose chief explorations are conducted from the town bench as they greet each passerby with preconceptions, personal history, and a biased pretense of detachment. Osborn, the most likeable and the one who eventually accompanies Todd to the *Floating Opera* performance, has the most profound effect on Andrews, because his complaining fulfillment is the most readily understood, and his hidden acceptance of life is paradoxically most attractive to the would-be suicide. Haecker, like Todd, suffers from being an intellectual, even if his wrongheaded argument for living contradicts his real despair at the ravages of an aging and purposeless existence. Even though Todd momentarily saves Haecker after a suicide attempt, Haecker's desire to end his life is no longer Todd's concern when Haecker later takes his own life in an institution. But despite his effort to philosophize his way into indifference, Todd cannot escape his perhaps irrational impulse to preserve life. We see this tendency early in the novel, during the scene when his father executes a chicken. Todd's own execution of the German in response to his consuming fear for his own life only reinforces this impulse. So disturbing is the elder Andrews's decision to commit suicide that Todd devotes much of his own remaining life to the search for a reason, and its relation to his own psyche.

All of the interlocking subplots and characters mesh together in the grand finale, the *Floating Opera*'s evening program, at once a reflection of everything else in the book and a reminder of the reflexive aspect of authorship that will inform all the rest of Barth's work. *The Floating Opera* is simultaneously the title of the book, the title of the showboat, the title of the showboat's entertainment, the metaphor for life as represented by the novel, and a blueprint for Barth's future fictional work. The surname of the owner/captain, Jacob R. Adam, suggests God's original imitation of his own image, and the given name is shared by Barth's second protagonist/author-surrogate, Jacob Horner, in *The End of the Road*. We have already noted the relationships among Captain Adam's vessel, Andrews's boats, and Barth's literary products.

The reader is also aware that the show has been billed as the climax of the novel, but that the impending but never realized cataclysm Todd has planned for his suicide never comes off—or Todd wouldn't be alive to write the book. As is the case with audiences for the Greek epics, our foreknowledge of the eventual outcome shifts our attention and suspense from what the outcome will be to why and how it came about. This strategy emphasizes the artistic process, the technique and the variety of ways in which the explanation unfolds, rather than any traditionally satisfactory resolution of the plot. The formula serves Barth, whose continuing emphasis will be on narrative method rather than plot. While the closed or ordained ending scheme appealed to the Greeks, who believed in predetermination, it is also satisfactory to modern existentialists, for whom neither the measure of justice nor the satisfaction produced by an appeasing moral conclusion is of great importance.

The comic center of the book is of course the opera or show itself, which recapitulates and caricatures the rest of the book. The entertainment is billed not only as a "High-Water Mark of Mirth," but as a "Great Moral Show . . . Moral and Refined" (*FO* 77). Todd, an exceptionally moral man, spends years of his life pretending not to have morals, at least in any traditional sense. His other pretenses include bearing no particular love for the woman who has been driving him crazy, and having no particular moral reason for either killing the man in the foxhole or practicing law on behalf of people whose cases he finds interesting (*FO* 72). He assures us, "I insist upon my basic and ultimate irresponsibility" (*FO* 83), but we never see him arguing a case on the morally wrong side of the tracks. The bizarre and byzantine courses he chooses to win his cases have little or no inherent justice in them, but are really comic in their intricacies and seeming irrelevance either to reality or to any officially sanctioned standard of justice. Instead they play on the absurdities of human nature and the law to produce a suitably moral outcome. Comedy habitually has eschewed traditional morality, even while producing a morally appeasing outcome. Thus, Todd's opinions of how and why he does things may be taken as another absurd aspect of a black comic novel.

The opera advertisement follows the same comic tack, with the vessel billed as "America's Finest & Safest Floating Theatre" when Todd's plans would make it a death trap for hundreds. "The Mary Pickford of the Chesapeake," Miss Clara Mulloy, does not appear in the "Hilarious! . . . Heartwarming! . . . Moral!" act, "The Parachute Girl," but her counterpart does appear in Andrews's parallel text in the person of Betty June Gunter, who introduces the seventeen-year-old Todd to sex. What begins with Betty Jane's recitation of her own teenage romantic pulp story ends in her silently engaging in sexual intercourse with a crying, bleating, roaring, braying and, finally, laughing Todd. In the sequel, which occurs six years later, Betty Jane, now a Baltimore prostitute, silently attacks Todd by pouring alcohol on his genitals and hitting him with a bottle. Unable to articulate her anguish over her lost lover during their first encounter, or her rage during the second, Betty Jane simply goes for the metaphoric jugular.

In the counterpart act from the *Floating Opera* performance, the silent, "trimly corseted" Clara Mulloy has, according to Captain Adam, "caught a germ from someplace—must have been Crisfield, couldn't have been Cambridge—and I swear if she ain't got the laryngitis so bad she can't say a durn word!" (*FO* 229). And so the heartwarming, hilarious story of the parachute girl is never told on stage, but replaced by the "Famous Southern Tenor," T. Wallace Whittaker, who instead of singing "Pastoral Lays of the Corn & Cotton Fields," begins to recite "Scenes from the Bard," a collection of somber Shakespearean soliloquies about death. Whittaker's versified miscellany, culminating in Hamlet's "To be or not to be . . . ," mirrors Todd's dark ruminations throughout the day. Framed in the lights of the *Floating Opera* stage, before an unsophisticated country audience set for a minstrel show, the portentous Shakespearean grimness is totally out of place, and becomes the object of derision by the crowd, who throw pennies, laugh, and hoot Whittaker off the stage. The irony is that the crowd loves its own derisive participation in what it considers pompous solemnity. There should be a lesson in it for Todd, who throws his change at Whittaker along with the rest. Todd's mental floating opera, featuring his own dark thoughts of the frivolousness of morality, will ultimately be the stuff of black humor, black thoughts garbed in popular comedy, the grim but hilarious formula for many of Barth's works to follow.

Next, the Ethiopian Tidewater Minstrels line up in a row, like the old men of the Explorers' Club, swapping stories, discussing the people and the world passing in front of them, and putting those caricatures into the minstrels' comic/tragic frame of reference. Todd describes the minstrel characters in the racist, sexist terms in which they were seen by the audience, while at the same time revealing the audience's dislike of the assumed education and cultivation of the learned interlocutor, played by the chameleon Todd surrogate, Captain Adam, whose role change from regular good old boy to educated, articulate master of ceremonies is so complete that no one can tell which role is authentic. Todd is, of course, the interlocutor of the Explorers' park bench, and may be defensive about his educated, detached reaction to the things the Explorers and the rest of the town hold sacred.

During the course of the minstrels' cogitations, the crowd on *The Floating Opera* is treated to the popular sentimental ballads of Sweet Sally Starbuck, whose "Melodies of Heart, Hearth, & Home" put the professed domestic bliss of her counterpart, Jane Mack, into a new comic, satiric light. Sweet Sally's offerings are followed by the comic preaching of J. Strudge, the Magnificent Ethiopian Delineator, the Black Demosthenes, whose comically cited text, *"Blessed am dem dat 'specks nuffin', 'caze dey ain't gwine git nuffin!,"* is a black comic version of Haecker's argument urging sweet acceptance of life's paltry gifts, followed by his attempt to kill himself.

The last act of the show consists of Burley Joe Wells's imitations. Burley Joe's act portrays some of the same qualities exhibited by burly Harrison Mack Jr., whose feeble, failed, misunderstanding attempts to imitate Todd's own misguided philosophies-in-progress inaugurate the years of pain and suffering of the *ménage à trois*. Burley Joe's steamboat-explosion imitation, which provides the climax of the show and the novel, is a realistic fabrication of a disaster, from which illusion the gullible audience recovers only after the entire troupe assures them with a final chorus that it was all part of the show. Burley Joe's explosion, which seemed so real, was, after all, only the clever fabrication of a talented performer.

Barth recapitulates the troupe's comforting finale with a denouement accomplishing much the same mollifying purpose. Todd's rationalization about the freedom not to commit suicide, the Explorers' chorus, the Mack family's final trio, and so on, all set the world and the company's decisions to rights—tying the ends together satisfactorily and with more existential consistency than the original printed version allowed it to have. The climactic reiteration of the showboat parallel reminds us that the whole novel and all its ideas are an artifice, a floating opera concocted by a new and highly original showman, who would go on to make even more ingenious use of the old, exhausted artistic forms to bring together audience and artifice into new relationships in new and even better shows.

NOTES

1. Todd claims he has known about his myocardial infarction "since 1919: thirty-five years" (*FO* 5). The sum of the two would make the time of writing 1954.
2. Charles B. Harris, *Passionate Virtuosity: The Fiction of John Barth* (Urbana: University of Illinois Press, 1983), pp. 17–18, 30n15.
3. Richard Schickel, "*The Floating Opera,*" *Critique* 6, no. 2 (Fall 1963): 58.
4. Ibid., p. 62.
5. Ibid., p. 63.
6. The conclusion of all reprinted editions (including the text followed in this study) follows the version Barth had originally intended to print. When Appleton-Century-Crofts agreed to be the original publisher they attached a condition: that Barth change the ending to make Todd appear more humane. David Morrell (*John Barth: An Introduction* [University Park: Pennsylvania State University Press], p. 7) describes the original Appleton-Century-Crofts ending this way:

Todd went backstage and switched on the gas jets as before, but then he remained backstage waiting to die of asphyxiation. Barth had literally fixed the book so that it ended not with a bang but a whimper: as Todd sat listening to the gas and smelling it, he was distracted by muffled voices in the next room. It seems a little girl who was perhaps his daughter had taken a convulsion while watching the show and was being carried backstage; and in his concern for her safety, Todd found a reason to keep himself alive.

Critics, agreeing with Barth's own assessment of the revision, thought it badly sentimental, and when the reprint rights were sold to Doubleday, Barth returned to his original plan.

2

Mythoscriptotherapy: *The End of the Road* and the Novel of Ideas

What would prompt a new novelist to use the same basic plot situation in his first two published works? According to David Morrell, *The End of the Road* had its repetitive drawbacks for Barth's original publisher, Appleton-Century-Crofts, who at least wanted to hold the manuscript for a while, since it was produced during the last three-month period of 1955, the same year in which Barth wrote *The Floating Opera* during January, February, and March.[1] Clearly, basic plot situations were mostly a vehicle for Barth's discussion of the philosophy and ideas underlying them. He hadn't said enough in his "nihilistic comedy," *The Floating Opera*, and he wanted to add the opposite dimension to his announced series about nihilism in his "nihilistic tragedy," *The End of the Road*.[2] Not until *Sabbatical* and *Tidewater Tales* would Barth replicate an earlier plot in a second book, although his entire oeuvre makes reference to his earlier works.

The Floating Opera and *The End of the Road* are centered around similar triangles, neither one totally realistic, but each representative of allegorical tableaux depicting ethical positions (rather than characters) in opposition to each other.[3] Nearly every principal character in the two novels pays homage to a nihilistic, schizoid vision of the sort that brings Todd to pay his room rent on a daily basis even though longer-term rental is cheaper (he has lived at his hotel for years), and Jake to dream of phoning the weather bureau to learn that there will be no weather the next day.

In *The End of the Road* Jake's philosophical position is set against the equally zany nihilism of Joe Morgan, whose *tabula rasa* wife, Rennie, renounced all claims to an identity before her marriage to Joe. Absolute freedom for Joe constitutes pimping her off to Jake to study their reactions and his own, claiming that the key to the free life is to conduct it unfettered by tradition, custom, or marital proprietorship. The same situation obtained in *The Floating Opera* with Harrison Mack and his wife. Jake's own philosophical stance has led him further toward the void than Todd's, however, since he is found by his therapist-in-waiting to be totally immobilized by graduate school and life in general, not knowing where to go, and sitting catatonic in a bus station, a victim of what the Doctor describes as "cosmopsis," a nihilistic world view that renders choice or action irrelevant, and therefore impossible.

Characters' names (or the lack of them) play a large role in these early books: Todd, a variant of the Germanic *tod*, or "death," and Jake Horner, calling to mind the nursery rhyme character who sits in a corner and the adulterer of William Wycherley's *The Country Wife*. Critics have also seen in Jacob's name the pragmatic and dissembling thief of Isaac's blessing. The most enigmatic character in *The End of the Road*, the Doctor, is, however, never named, in keeping with his mysterious, trickster-figure nature. To accentuate the Doctor's otherness, Barth made him a black man and refused, after some public-relations reluctance by publishers fearing charges of racism, to change him into a Caucasian.[4] A combination of parodies of God, Sartre, and Heidegger,[5] the Doctor makes a living curing the angst of a set of jealous but nearly immobilized patients who inhabit his probably illegal premises. Like the other principal male characters in the book, the Doctor too is a nihilist, but a pragmatic one. Having long since given up the idea, at least with Jake, that there is a right or even reasonable way to act in any given set of circumstances, he counsels the arbitrary, just so a decision is made. His Farm is, after all, a place of Remobilization, the title itself expressing action. Practicing what he preaches, the Doctor is alone in the local medical community in his willingness to perform an abortion on Rennie. It is the pragmatic choice, and seems to be the result of a good deal he made in exchange for Jake's indefinite service to the Farm.

The description of the Doctor's Progress and Advice Room and its furniture arrangement is a comic parody of a situation designed to force positional and spatial responses from the patient. Jake is advised to take a job teaching prescriptive grammar at Wicomico State Teachers College, the name suggesting a combination of the comic aspect of the Wye River (Wye/comic), which will figure prominently in the later novels, the comic side of the Y or crotch (Y/comic—again a pun in later books), and, finally, the question of why nihilism has to be represented only in the comic manner of *The Floating Opera* (Why comic, O[pera]?).

The Doctor prescribes impulsive action, admonishing Jake:

Don't get stuck between alternatives, or you're lost. . . . If the alternatives are side by side, choose the one on the left; if they're consecutive in time, choose the earlier. If neither of these applies, choose the alternative whose name begins with the earlier letter of the alphabet. (*ER* 85)

Jake's indecision is to be assuaged by teaching the most rigorous form of articulation, prescriptive grammar, and inventing an equally arbitrary set of masks as models for living, roles he can change at will, the adoption of which is called mythotherapy. The therapies the Doctor orders are all extreme, near comic in nature. Invent your personality and change it at will, the Doctor orders, implying that Jake possesses no predesignated or even evolving dominant mental predisposition; and if that therapy doesn't work, make your decisions arbitrarily. When all that fails, try scriptotherapy—set down something resembling your experiences in an arbitrary, grammar-dominated language, forcing experience into an unreal artistic mold. It is presumably scriptotherapy that prompts Jake to write the book two years after the events he narrates purportedly took place.

The relationship of the novel Jake eventually produces to the action is a major factor in any attempt to understand what *The End of the Road* is all about. Is the book merely a scriptotherapeutic artifice? Is it really believable, since many of the events and opinions seem so bizarre as to defy credibility? Yet other scenes, such as the death of Rennie, choking on her regurgitated supper under anesthesia, seem frighteningly real. The principal characters themselves seem otherworldly, dominated by abstract philosophical principles, like Joe Morgan, or lack of conviction, like Jake Horner. These two avatars of conflicting existential philosophies represent completely reasoned activism on Joe's part and a kind of nihilism on Jake's.

Joe Morgan, who seeks a rational answer for everything, is governed solely by his drive to understand completely his own actions as well as those of his wife and the people around him. He is driven by his zany logic to the point of putting Rennie in sexual jeopardy by throwing her into an extramarital situation with Jake Horner. Joe tests the will, actions, and morality of all three in engineering the means of Rennie and Jake's infidelity, so that he can have the perverted pleasure of mentally dissecting their responses and his own. The least believable part of his action is that he seems mystified that adultery could occur at all. Outwardly Joe is a model teacher and faculty colleague, intelligent, apparently honest, and hard working. The weakest link in his twisted psyche is his irrational other. He is caught by Rennie and Jake executing military commands "cavorting about the room," wildly gyrating and making faces at himself in the mirror, babbling, and picking his nose while masturbating. The discovery is a crucial moment for Rennie, who had always viewed her husband as a paragon. Joe's arrested development is foreshadowed by his association with the Boy Scouts, his seeming inability to complete his dissertation, and his lack of insight into his own subconscious motivations. The image of masturbating Boy Scout executing military commands sums up his antirational side, which can't be stifled by the higher abstractions of reason. Presumably even Jake believes in Joe's zany facade as cuckolded Boy Scout when Jake confesses, "He never looked finer or stronger to me than at that moment when I thought of him at the Boy Scout meeting" (*ER* 103). Anyone on an English faculty for any length of time will recognize this sort of damaging, berserk brilliance, only a breath removed from burlesque behavior.

Jake's position on practically every issue is to see both sides of any situation, and to avoid either making judgments or being paralyzed by having to make decisions. With no overweening certainty about anything or any mode of conduct, Jake is, from the first line of the book ("IN A SENSE, I AM JACOB HORNER"), not totally certain of his own identity. The Doctor's therapy of having Jake choose any arbitrary set of standards devalues every value system into meaninglessness. Even the scriptotherapy of writing the book, certainly an arduous enough task, is an assigned exercise, just as running on a treadmill is an arbitrary exercise: It merely keeps you going. Jake has an affinity for the arbitrary, however. His pursuit of a job teaching *pre*scriptive grammar in an age when *de*scriptive grammar is the fad of preference appeals to his sense of the worthlessness of everything which might be arbitrary. A grammar based on Latin applied to a Teutonic language doesn't begin to come to grips with the reality of a dynamic, evolving, live language, as Jake well knows. Prescriptive grammar is like Joe's pure reason: It can't fully comprehend human verbalization, and skews the reality of spontaneous speech. Jake demonstrates the hopeless rationality of prescriptive grammar in his class discussion. His dislike of its very falsity and arbitrariness is clear from his prescriptive responses to a student who objects. Like any sophist/teacher, he can lay waste the unwashed undergraduate, but the discipline is only Jake's method of controlling the subliminal forces that continually threaten to overwhelm him.

Jake, like Joe, has a sexual Achilles' heel. The description of the first day of class is a dramatic, hilarious departure in style and reserve from the rest of the book:

The boys, too, lean and green, smooth-chinned and resilient, shivered and stretched at the mere nearness of young breasts and buttocks as hard as new pears. In a classroom on the first day of a new term the air's electric with sex like ozone after a summer storm, and all sensed it, if all couldn't name it; the rubby sweet friskies twitched in their seats and tugged their skirts down dimpled white knees . . . little's to be done but nod to Freud on such a day. (*ER* 94)

It is temptation enough for Jake to seek out Peggy Rankin. When he finds her still amenable to his advances, he plays a Joe to Peggy's Rennie as he socks Peggy in the Morgan fashion and gives Peggy essentially the same line Joe has been dishing out to his wife. After spending an entire day at school in libidinous heat, Jake hypocritically tells Peggy he is "*just not that interested* in laying women" (*ER* 97), and then his ultimate ploy of hitting her to prove he takes her seriously finally brings her to bed. He cynically admits, "I made a mental salute to Joseph Morgan, *il mio maestro*, and another to Dr. Freud, caller of the whole comic hoedown" (*ER* 97).

Charles Harris finds Jake's posture of narrator/author a schizoid tendency, with Jake stepping outside himself to observe his own actions, just as Joe has essentially stepped outside his marriage to afford himself a detached understanding of how he reacted to his wife's adultery. Jake's reliance on language in art (fiction) is for Harris[6] an arbitrary attempt to simplify and freeze human nature into stable reason, assimilate it into a rational framework, and then reintroduce it to the outside world in the form of a chronicle. Joe's failure to finish his dissertation is an admission of his own inability to do the same thing.

In *The End of the Road* Barth begins to define a technique he uses throughout his entire canon: exploring philosophical positions by carrying them to their extreme but logical conclusions—taking them to the end of the road—and in the process expanding them into satiric parodies. One of his consistent topics is the act of writing a fiction that discusses its own creation. Joe attempts to live as if he were scripting a fiction based on existentialist reason, and in the process involves an impressionable, reborn wife who will participate in his experiment without prior intellectual defenses, and a colleague who can't seem to make up his mind about anything. Little they do makes rational sense. Jake, who isn't even sure of his own existence and knows little or nothing about what enervates as well as motivates him, finds himself forced into purposeful action by the circumstances of Rennie's threatened suicide. In the end it is not reason, choice, or creative planning that dictates the tragedy of her death, but arbitrary circumstance and the Doctor's ineptitude and lack of precautions.

Since the main characters' mind-sets, reasoning, and circumstances often defy credibility as realism, the story lends itself to an allegorical cast, and one of the most popular with critics is the Garden of Eden motif. Several Barth scholars, including Herbert Smith, see Joe as a reasoning Godlike figure[7] or an Adam figure, while Rennie, or Eve, is tempted by the serpent,

Jake. One of the difficulties with this scenario is that the Morgan marriage can hardly be described as Edenic, based as it is on Rennie's mindless appreciation of Joe's punches and her veneration of his peerless insight. Then too, Jake's indecision, albeit occasionally mitigated by his sexual libido, hardly constitutes any sort of ego-driven Satanic rebellion or premeditated attempt to overthrow the Morgan marital paradise. Nevertheless, the two unsuspecting existentialists are in a competition, which neither will recognize, over the body/soul/mind of Rennie, and the result of her own simpleminded innocence is her death. It happens not through her own volition (like her threatened suicide), but because she chokes when regurgitating the sauerkraut and hot dogs she has eaten, like the self-destructive ideologies or nonideologies that choke all three characters in the end. It is the pretense of normality, eating and living an accustomed, mundane life in the midst of lunatic rationality, that finally does her in.

The most intriguing character in the book, the nameless Doctor, is linked with power, despite his surface submission to and battles with the authorities. He possesses an undefined relationship with chaos, an affinity with the forces that move human lives. Yet he seems, because of his own dilemmas and zany ideas, to have an almost comic, Mephisthophelean streak. He is close enough to the bizarre to be a forerunner of those semidemonic trickster figures Burlingame and Bray, who will dominate *The Sot-Weed Factor*, *Giles Goat-Boy*, and *LETTERS*.

In *The End of the Road* the Doctor is more like a caricature of a God who espouses the arbitrary, sees no ultimate good in any creed but the practical, and ends by participating in the clumsy chaos that dominates the world of events he has set in motion. His pronouncement on Rennie's death is, "What a mess this is" (*ER* 191). The closest figure in modern American fiction is Doctor T. J. Eckleburg, God of the Wasteland ashheap in *The Great Gatsby*, and his counterpart character, Owl Eyes, whose pronouncement on Gatsby after the funeral service—"The poor son-of-a-bitch"—is like the sympathy of a remote and nearly helpless disempowered deity.

In developing his trickster figures, Barth writes in a satiric tradition that complements but runs counter to those lovable, innocent, if slightly sanctimonious mentors of the eighteenth-century burlesques of reason and morality, *Candide*'s Pangloss and *Tom Jones*'s Parson Adams. The black doctor is, according to E. P. Walkiewicz, another *philosophus gloriosis*, dominating patients with his half-baked egocentricities.[8] Their worldly or otherworldly advice lands his eighteenth-century counterparts in messes as bad as the one in which the Doctor finds himself in chapter 12, but the grim details of Rennie's death hardly constitute a just reward for comic innocence.

The End of the Road is professedly something other than comic. In the earlier works the mentors were as simplistic and as sure of their notions about morality and reason as is Joe in his commitment to his existential activism, or Jake to his ennui, or the Doctor to his offbeat pragmatism, but the conclusions of the eighteenth-century works returned their readers to the conventional philosophic or moral convictions of their day, while Barth's plot leaves us with the existential nonanswers of the fifties. In one respect, the Mephistophelean Doctor does come out ahead. He has been bargaining for control over Jake's mind and body instead of his soul (which has by the twentieth century become virtually meaningless), and Jake surrenders both to the Doctor in agreeing to work on the relocated Rehabilitation Farm. The book is in itself a part of the debt exacted by the Doctor. Jake has apparently not derived any beneficial or therapeutic effect from writing the text: He still doesn't know if he really is Jake Horner, and his personal philosophy and survival are apparently still articulated for him in a Pepsi Cola jingle and in his identification with the bust of Laocoön, the powerless doomed profaner of the temple and the unheeded prophet of the Greek's gift horse. Jake's affinity to the bust on his mantel is explained in the conclusion: "The terrific incompleteness made me volatile; my muscles screamed to act; but my limbs were bound like Laocoön's—by the serpents Knowledge and Imagination, which, grown great in the fullness of time, no longer tempt but annihilate" (*ER* 196). Jake's totem figure of inaction is left on his mantel as he climbs into the taxi to get to the bus headed for the Doctor's new farm. His direction for the driver, "Terminal," is the last word in the book, and an obvious message that things are not going to get any better for Jake.

The End of the Road is, then, a sort of *Künstlerroman* of inactivity and hopelessness, a record of the lessons of a young novelist learning about the pointlessness of life and the futility of any attempt to construct a system of reason that would comprehend it. Jake, as narrator, calls our attention to the fact that he has shortened or condensed some scenes and speeches to suit his own aesthetic ends, leading us to wonder how much of the material he has simply made up or omitted. Are the flaws of the narrator the same as those of the main character, especially if they are one and the same? If the message is as meaningless as the world of Jake Horner seems to be, then the question doesn't make much difference. The object was to explore the nihilistic mind-set, as the title suggests, to the end of the road.

NOTES

1. David Morrell, *John Barth: An Introduction* (University Park: Pennsylvania State University Press, 1976), pp. 13–14.

2. Ibid., p. 13.

3. Herbert F. Smith, "Barth's Endless Road," *Critique* 6, no. 2 (1963): 68–69.

4. John Enck, "John Barth: An Interview," *Wisconsin Studies in Contemporary Literature* 6 (Winter-Spring 1965): 12.

5. Smith, p. 70.

6. Charles B. Harris, *Passionate Virtuosity: The Fiction of John Barth* (Urbana: University of Illinois Press, 1983), p. 47.

7. Smith, p. 72.

8. E. P. Walkiewicz, *John Barth* (Boston: Twayne, 1986), p. 37.

3

The New *Marylandiad*: Barth as Poet Laureate in *The Sot-Weed Factor*

The Sot-Weed Factor represents a dramatic departure from Barth's first two novels in tone, substance, and intent. That does not mean that Barth abandoned his earlier philosophical positions or his sense of absurdity. Rather, *Sot-Weed* reflects expanded ambitions as well as startling technical virtuosity, and a rich vein of comic ribaldry that evidenced itself earlier in such scenes as Jake's first day in class and Joe's solitary antics in *The End of the Road* and the lawsuit over old Mack's excrement in *The Floating Opera*. *Sot-Weed* required a new, far larger canvas than the previous short novels to fulfill Barth's ambition to reinterpret the early history of Maryland, the eighteenth-century novel, the philosophy of the Age of Reason, a big chunk of classical mythology, and most of the epic canon. In short, in attempting a contemporary redefinition of the essence of colonial Maryland, Barth also took on the task of providing a new version of the modern history of Western man.[1]

Appropriating Henry Fielding's language and imitations of earlier literary forms, types, and genres, Barth combined eighteenth-century literature with archival history as the primary elements of ingenious transformations by which he intended to correct America's view of its own history and to forge a relationship between modern history and literature, art, and perception. Such a grand scheme involved the young author in writing himself and his own creative struggle into the book. Barth's goals were not dissimilar to Ebenezer Cooke's: to frame a new *Marylandiad* for an area which, unlike William Faulkner's South, Carl Sandburg's Midwest, or Henry David Thoreau's New England, lacked any literary-historical definition except for the original Ebenezer Cooke poem, "The Sot-Weed Factor," published in London in 1708. In a sense Barth tries to account for the biting satire of

Cooke's poem, the story behind its unflattering dissimilarity to the panegyrics of Rome in *The Aeneid* or of Elizabethan England in *The Faerie Queene*. In doing so he offers an original, zany interpretation of such existing records as the journals of Captain John Smith and William Byrd, the Maryland archives, and a biography of Cooke by Lawrence Wroth, published by the American Antiquarian Society in 1934.[2] Critics, led by David Morrell,[3] have gone to some lengths to demonstrate that Barth never violated the letter of the historical facts as stated in the archives. He did, however, take monstrous liberties in interpretation, and, in short, presented a Barthean version of American history in all its infamous and antic detail, while at the same time calling readers' attention to the confusion of fiction with history, and art with interpretation.

To emphasize the confusion, the outcome of Barth's novel and the compositional riddle of Cooke's poem hinge on the recovery of four conflicting segments of two opposing narrative points of view: the journals of Captain John Smith, whose published accounts of his explorations of America have discrepancies among their various editions, and the opposing accounts of his fictional lieutenant/rival, Henry Burlingame I, whose own biases, while altering the meaning of Smith's exploits, fill in missing narrative details. Together these accounts provide the key to the novel—the eggplant recipe, the discovery of which is the answer not only to Burlingame's past, but to the future of the Burlingame progeny and the course of colonial history.

In writing a history that corresponds to known, archivally documented facts and events, yet that differs so radically from accepted versions of what transpired, especially in the interpretation of the documents themselves, Barth casts doubt on what we, as Americans, have always been taught to consider the rosy historical basis of our own heritage. Such a debunking of historical encomia was presumably one of the aims of Ebenezer Cooke, when, in the eighteenth century, he sought to provide a satiric corrective to the roseate portraits of the New World. Barth, serving as Cooke's modern successor, seeks to elaborate on Cooke's poem, providing fanciful details explaining how Cooke arrived at such a sour view of his new world, and in the process revives and revitalizes the history of America. In this attempt Barth's novel resembles James Joyce's unflattering portraits of Irish and particularly Dublin life and people in such works as *Dubliners*, *A Portrait of the Artist as a Young Man*, and *Ulysses*. Writing at a time that made heavy political demands on Ireland's artists to produce sympathetic, glorifying portraits of the Irish citizenry, Joyce instead, like John Millington Synge and Sean O'Casey, wrote of their meanness, and that of the institutions that ruled them. Ironically, it is these portraits, with their ring of verisimilitude, that attract scholars and general readers to Ireland and its people, as even the Irish Tourist Board is now willing to acknowledge. What these writers did for Ireland went far beyond wholesome propaganda. Unflattering or not, their portrayals link a great and believable people with the unforgettable art that realistically portrayed them. Similarly, Cooke and Barth may well have brought colonial Maryland and its citizens into fanciful, and at the same time ultimately believable, focus in ways that no historical panegyrics would ever be able to accomplish.

As Barth tells us in the concluding pages of the denouement, Cooke's poem, with all its fashionable comic satire, had an effect on literate eighteenth-century British society, in that it attracted them to Maryland, not as a primitive, uncivilized society, but as a place where culture and refinement were understood and appreciated. The sophisticated demands satire makes on its readers also imply membership in a cultural or intellectual upper class, whose participation is self-selecting and flattering at the same time. This pious truth applies to Barth readers as well as Enlightenment sophisticates.

Most persons who are not forced into reading *The Sot-Weed Factor* as part of a long and difficult class syllabus take delight in Barth for the same reasons earlier readers appreciated Cooke. We have always suspected that the party line on the brave, self-sacrificing fathers of our country rang about as true as the one about the freedom-loving Kuwaitis of the Gulf War. Our love of seeing official versions of history debunked sometimes leads us to the error of making excessive claims for the debunker. Barth's book, with its technical virtuosity and command of literary, historical, and mythic predecessors, has few rivals among contemporary novels, and *Sot-Weed*'s reputation among many highly literate modern readers is analogous to the popularity—according to the narrator—of Cooke's satire in eighteenth-century literary society. Leslie Fiedler, whose own historical indignation and linguistic inventiveness were stimulated by Barth, sees him as "an existentialist comedian suffering history, not just because it happens to be *à la mode* to be comic and existentialist, but because, born in Maryland in his generation and reborn in graduate school, he can scarcely afford to be anything else."[4] Fiedler seizes on the comic aspects of *Sot-Weed* to establish its place in the American canon: "The book is a joke-book, an endless series of gags. But the biggest joke of all is that Barth seems finally to have written something closer to the 'Great American Novel' than any other book of the last decades."[5] The points to be made are several: that two centuries have not changed our perceptions of fiction and history as a continuum of metaphors from whose comic mixture we can ultimately derive some intuitive truth; and that Barth, in writing his own version of the *Mary-*

landiad, has self-consciously become the modern Ebenezer Cooke, writing a modernist/existentialist colonial history.

Other personal parallels between Barth and Cooke include Barth's intimate knowledge of the Chesapeake Bay area, in which most of the action takes place; the multiplicity of ambivalent but strong feelings between male and female twins, which apply to Barth's early inseparability from his twin sister Jill as much as they do to Anna and Eben; the proximity of Barth's home to Malden; and the vast scope of both Eben's and Barth's ultimately revisionist literary pretensions.

Having chosen an actual minor eighteenth-century satiric text on which to base his novel and actual historical texts against which to frame it, Barth chose as his principal literary objects of parody the novels of Henry Fielding. In one of his most frequently cited quotations Barth concedes that he set out "to see if I couldn't make up a plot that was fancier than *Tom Jones*."[6] Fielding's long, convoluted picaresque novels, such as the one Barth singled out, have the reputation for tying the loose ends of all the subplots together in a conclusion so fraught with coincidence as to implicitly announce the work an artifice rather than the faithful recording of history it initially represented itself to be. To subtitle any account "A True Historie" was to invite skepticism, especially in a comic work.

Fielding's road adventures are part of a long literary tradition, including the earliest novels by Cervantes and Rabelais, and, even further back, the works of Dante, Virgil, and Homer. *The Odyssey* and *The Divine Comedy*, especially, consist heavily of narratives by diverse storytellers, all contributing to or bearing intimately upon the main purpose or history of the frame story. Barth, as usual, pushed the tradition to the point of burlesque. Charles Harris's discussion of the variety of narratives and narrators in *Sot-Weed* outlines four segments of the two conflicting versions of history by Smith and Burlingame as being at the center of the novel, while no less than twenty-five interpolated narratives related by seventeen different narrators are all intertwined as bearing on Burlingame's family ties, Eben's history, and their quests for a past or a future.[7]

Barth's scheme depended in part on the axiom that nothing comes out perfectly. The fulfillment of his grandiose claim to resolve every loose end of every plot complication by the end of the book implied a novel pleasing by way of artistic contrivance, rather than an account conveying realistic believability. The effect was to call attention to Barth's artifice as a conscious imitation of Fielding's artifice, while at the same time both works attempted to retain the attitude of truth generated by satiric debunking. In this Barth was, of course, seconded by other literary predecessors who shared his belief that recorded history is simply a creative narration in disguise. Shakespeare's recreation of the history of England's monarchy is in many ways as creative an account as Virgil's history of the founding of Rome.

The essence or meaning of reality, *the facts*, lies in something other than a pretense of neutral literal recital. Few academics outside the sciences now believe that total neutrality or objectivity is possible, because any account is always couched in language shaped by its narrator. The meaning of external events—what we call reality—lies in their metaphoric value, or what they represent other than themselves, and this value is established only by the artistry of their translation, no matter how pedestrian its nature. That artistry may be political or commercial as well as literary.

Barth's subject matter is not only colonial history and the way it affects its *Künstlerroman* protagonist, but a celebration of the poetry and fiction that metaphorize history—of the way they transform events into meaningful images. His method involves proclaiming rather than concealing the derivative nature of his work, glorying in his place in the long line of literary precursors. *Sot-Weed* trumpets the succession through direct reference as well as imitation and borrowing from writers throughout Western literary tradition, including not only such diverse paradigms as those already mentioned, but others like Laurence Sterne, Voltaire, Goethe, Plato, John Bunyan, René Descartes, and Friedrich Wilhelm Nietzsche, to name only a few of the most recognizable. If the tradition has come to a point of exhaustion of idea and artifice, then Barth's celebratory imitation is its replenishment. To reinvigorate former artistic glory is analogous to revitalizing history, as both forms vie for the contemporary imagination.

The context of the literary history out of which Barth writes includes his own two previous novels. Barth's concern with nihilism prevented either of his first two books from being a pure *Bildungsroman*, but there are aspects of the genre in Jake Horner's narrative. The protagonists of Barth's first three novels are all chroniclers, their composition part of their scriptotherapy, as expressions of their search for identity or meaning in life. Sex plays a major role in all of Barth, and especially sexual rivalry in his first three books. For the first-person narrators women assume metaphorical identities as both muses and temptresses. Todd's self-destructive tendencies are in some measure dependent on his rivalry with Harrison Mack over Jane Mack, a motif that would be continued in the triangle involving Jake Horner and the Morgans, and expanded into a rivalry of intellectual philosophies in *The End of the Road*. Barth again uses the *Künstlerroman* form to complement the sexual-competition motif elaborated in *Sot-Weed*, which features rivalries between Burlingame and Ebenezer and Eben and Billy Rumbly over Anna; between Eben and McEvoy and Eben and Captain

Mitchell (among an army of others) over Joan Toast; and other assorted rivalries developed in the subplots.

While Eben's love for Joan Toast begins as a social-philosophical dispute with his innocent romanticizing of both their chastity, on one hand, and her hard-headed businesslike bargaining, on the other, both views are modified by the end. Joan's pimp/lover McEvoy is an honest whorebroker, a fair but also naïve follower of fair business ethics. Ultimately he becomes Eben's most dependable male ally. Despite McEvoy's practical sense of the worthlessness of altruistic exposure to danger, his ethical consciousness leads him to share Eben's risks even though they imperil his own life. Joan eventually sacrifices her future, her health, and finally her life for the pure romantic devotion she eschewed in her initial precoital encounter with Eben. Yet she retains some dignity for her philosophy by demanding the last whore/price of her estate for a sound swiving.

Building on the rivalry for Rennie's mind as well as body between competing existential values—Joe's irrational rationality and Jake's hopeless resignation—in *The End of the Road*, the rivalries among Eben and two of the Burlingame brothers over Anna represent a greater spectrum of issues involving political and social philosophy. Henry, the cynical mentor, is a shape-changing *carpe diem* advocate who eschews moral restraint for the amoral vitality of action, while his brother, Billy Rumbly, is obsessed with the relation between social responses and morality. Unable, by dint of Henry's physical shortcomings, to take the most expedient (copulative) course of action in consummating her devotion to him, Anna relegates him for most of the book to an erotic if technically chaste relationship. Rumbly, with the same physical deficiencies as his brother, is further burdened by a schizophrenic identity socially split between English cultivation and noble savagery. Anna embraces Billy's savagery, while Billy embraces English social culture. When she chooses Eben and her own heritage, he reverts to his own.

Henry, almost elevated to the importance of co-protagonist in the book, shares his ingenuity, intellectual and scholarly capacity, impulsiveness, and romantic *Sturm und Drang* attitudes, as well their mutually diminutive genitalia, with his two brothers, Charley Mattessin and Billy Rumbly. In a sense they are composites, resembling each other mentally as well as physically, but with accents on varying aspects of social and philosophical identity. Each is identified with some aspect of Eben's own behavior: naïveté, strong and highly individualistic senses of morality, disinterest in monetary acquisition, and ability to take decisive action at great risk.

In *The End of the Road* Jake Horner had to be forced into action, first by the Doctor, then by Joe Morgan's orchestrated triangle, and then by the plight of the victimized Rennie. Rennie's sacrifice for another's ideas parallels Joan Toast's, as both are caught up in the irrationality of seemingly rational ideals. Joe's role as Boy Scout leader and his masturbatory antics prefigure Billy Rumbly, the original native boy scout with bizarre personal behavior and pretensions of sophistication, as Barth continues to pursue questions he raised in the earlier works.

Henry Burlingame is more than merely Eben's chief rival. Barth expands the role of the mysterious black Doctor in *The End of the Road* into that of a full-blown dark-side trickster-figure who acts as mentor to spur the lethargic or "cosmopsis"-beset protagonist to act, even in ways that seem completely arbitrary, simply for the sake of taking action and making choices. Burlingame, like his predecessor, has acquired some sort of special self-possession that proclaims an intimate knowledge of the way the world functions, and of the dark forces that control it. In practicing what he preaches, Burlingame fulfills the shape-changing role of the mythic trickster archetype. Like the Doctor, he has a rational explanation and an outside view of the world at odds with society's standards and ideas, and he urges his student/patient, Eben, out of lethargy and into action for its own sake.

The shape of Eben's destiny is not entirely molded by his tutor, however, but also by Joan Toast's generation of his romantic reaction to his own libidinous impulses. Eben's beatification of a whore and dedication to a celibate poetic pursuit worthy of her image have all sorts of courtly love precedents, none more obvious than *Don Quixote*. The resolution of her poxed, diseased, oft-swived, and oft-abused fate—in which she proves to be as worthy as he thinks she is—is brought about by her adopting Eben's dreams, much as the La Mancha crowd apparently does just before the Don's death. Short of ascension into sainthood, she would have been far better off, physically if not spiritually, sharing life with her honest but practical pimp, McEvoy.

The Sot-Weed Factor and Barth's next book, *Giles Goat-Boy*, share common ground in the author's concentration on the problems of literary creativity as well as philosophical speculation. While both concerns are evident enough in all Barth's works, the emphasis shifts by *Lost in the Funhouse* to the act of writing itself and problems concerned with the relationship of author and text. The focus of *Sot-Weed* changes from the protagonist's chronicling events merely to understand them. Instead, *Sot-Weed* represents Barth's first attempt to make a new form of literature rather than a traditional text merely depicting a psychological or philosophical problem. While *Sot-Weed* does contain elements of "scriptotherapy," it concerns itself more directly with literary criticism, and it represents the problems encountered by its protagonist in creating an epic poem for a literary audience.

As we have already seen, unlike previous Barth books, *Sot-Weed* is parodic, using previous literary texts to create a new and viable work about literary composition itself. Of course, Barth never really lets go of a metaphor or idea, as we will see in discussion of future texts, although the scope of each increases even as the emphasis shifts. Eben's goal of writing an epic poem about the history and essence of his new country carries the freight of *The Aeneid*; writing a sea-journey/road adventure of return to recapture hearth and home, an *Odyssey*; writing a spiritual allegory undertaken at the instigation of a saintly woman, a *Divine Comedy*; writing a trip through carnality, flatulence, drunken debauchery, and the social follies of the age, a *Gargantua* and *Pantagruel*; writing a satire debunking the philosophical pretensions of the age, a *Candide*; and writing satire on social, moral, and literary pretensions, a *Don Quixote*, "Rape of the Lock," "Dunciad," *Tom Jones*, and "Hudibras." The enterprise did not lack a certain self-confidence.

Two self-conscious aspects of classical parody were farcical discussions of literary forms—such as those between Quixote and Panza on courtly romance—and exaggeration of the trivial to epic proportion by creating enormous lists of objects, examples, and activities—such as the advantages and disadvantages to Panurge's marriage in Rabelais, or the details of Uncle Toby's fortifications in Sterne. Few epic battles could rival the mock grandeur of the first Henry Burlingame's eating contest with Attonce for the kingship of the Ahatchwoops. The details of the preparations themselves take on comic magnificence:

Attonce then commenc'd to slapp his bellie with his hands, to the end he might arowse a grander lust for food, and seeing him, Burlingame did likewise, untill the rumbling of there guts did eckoe about the swamps like the thunder of vulcanoes. Next Attonce, sitting cross-legged, did bump his buttockes up & down upon the earthe, farther to appetyze him selfe; Burlingame also, that he give his foe no quarter, and the verie grownd shudder'd beneath there awful bummes. Burlingame then blubber'd his lipps & snapt the joynt-bones of his fingers, and Attonce likewise. Attonce op'd & shutt his jawes with great rapiditie, and also Burlingame. And thus they did goe on, through many a ceremonie, whetting there hungers, whilst our companie sat as amaz'd, not knowing what they witness'd and the Salvages clapt there hands & daunc'd about and Pokatawertussan look'd all lustilie from one to the other. (*SW* 597)

Often these epic lists and chroniclings take a Rabelaisian/Sternean literary bent, such as the whores' five-page contest (477–82) over how many names each could give for the plyers of their trade, or Eben's rhyming contest with Burlingame (415–16), or Burlingame/Sayer's discovery of unintended word plays in Eben's poetry (135), or Eben's exhaustive search through literary precedent for something resembling toilet paper to wipe himself with (188–90).

Barth compounds the literary comedy with aphorisms, dispensed not only by Eben, but by the most unlikely characters, such as Eben's duplicitous servant Bertrand, Mary Mungummory ("The Traveling Whore o' Dorset"), and a host of other nonliterary types. The concentration of language and literature, per se, defines the topic as a major concern of the book, not trivialized so much as raised to prominence by the comedic structure. The numerous discussions, debates, and scenes regarding the theory and practice of freedom of choice and general philosophic questions, both natural and ethical, lead to a parallel insistence on philosophic questions. Here again Barth draws on his own previous oeuvre as well as the classical canon when he turns the question of existential freedom, so paramount and often deadly serious in *The End of the Road*, into a hilarious multiplicity of choices regarding which kind of notebook to buy for his poetry manuscript (119–21).

In being so openly derivative, Barth knowingly violated verisimilitude of plot, structure, and characterization. Often accused by critics of lacking credible characters, or of a paucity of "well-rounded" characterization, Barth's books became increasingly formulaic, but never predictable. His first two books were the only preponderantly realistic novels he wrote, until he later returned to blending major doses of realism into the fictive stews of the books following *LETTERS*. In *Sot-Weed* Eben's unbelievable naïveté and Burlingame's equally incredible adroitness at dissembling remain true to their philosophy and the dictates of their literary forebears, but come off as less complex than his other ingenious intricacies of plot and originality of parody.

Satire, a far milder form of imitation than burlesque, still has the quality of exaggerating certain recognizable traits at the expense of others, the same way that comedy plays with exaggeration to the point of burlesque. *Sot-Weed*'s character development has it both ways, with characters realistically defined by their deeds, and their deeds by their overblown philosophies. This is not to say that Barth's characters are inflexible. Eben's final state of mind in rejecting the long sought Laureateship of Maryland, Joan Toast's acceptance of altruism in her whoredom, and McEvoy's self-sacrificial evolution from his earlier materialism are 180-degree turns from their original philosophical predispositions. But the basically "good," the morally ambivalent, and the "evil" characters remain that way throughout their ordeals, just as they do in the literature of the eighteenth century and before.

While forgivable human weaknesses pervade the virtue of Eben's artistic evangelism, Burlingame's persistent search for identity, the noble savagery of Burlingame's brothers and the enslaved African kings, and Father FitzMaurice's missionary zeal, their ultimate goodness is ratified by the counterbalancing machinations of politicians, judges, lawyers, and the clergy caught in the all-pervasive folly and unholy alliances of religious warfare and covetousness transported to the New World from the continent, along with its culture and literature.

It is hard to fault Mary Mungummory, Joan Toast, or the all-wise Governor Nicholson, who restores our faith in the ultimate intelligence, honesty, and integrity of the establishment. Conversely, such blackguards as Sly and the Miller are unredeemable. However, none of the characters is beset with the morally ambiguous dilemmas of Clytemnestra, Oedipus, or Willy Loman; instead, we are presented with situations for which their immoral or moral certitude or philosophical stances dictate the sorts of choices Barth's characters will make. That is why Burlingame plays such a decisive role in the novel. As trickster figure, Burlingame constantly calls upon the reader and Eben to try to fathom his moral convictions, despite Burlingame's constant assertion of his right to personal amorality in an amoral universe.

Still, given the parodic nature of the book, the blatant finality in Barth's tying up all loose ends implies a set of moral resolutions appeasing to both the modern and eighteenth-century versions of rational correctness. It is not enough to say that only a satirical farce could accommodate the ingeniousness of a complete resolution to the bewildering variety of plots. As sad or happy as the characters' situations are at the end, they must still be appropriate, and such appropriateness calls for moral sanction different from that in Barth's first two novels. Later works of Barth will be less stringent in their demand for moral resolution, but his parody of Fielding in *Sot-Weed* implies imitation of both substance and artifice.[8]

In assigning the roots of Ebenezer's and Henry's quests to sex, Barth went further back in literary history than the eighteenth century. His precedents include the sexual impetus for the Trojan War, the sexual possessiveness of *The Odyssey*, the sexual forbearance of Aeneas, the perverted sex-drive of Dante, the romanticism of Quixote, and the gonad-driven decision of Adam in *Paradise Lost*. Burlingame's search for a penis extension is the dark side of Eben's search for a monumental work of poetry to glorify and possess both whore and sister muses. The chronicle that produced the great eggplant artifice that bestows ultimate manhood on Burlingame is analogous to the poem which won Barth and Eben their respective niches in literary history. What nature can't endow, artifice can.

In creating the eggplant artifice, Barth makes still another variation on the phallic aphorism about whether the pen is mightier than the sword. The metonymical expansion of the diminutive pen(is) into a humongous, artistically created eggplant is an apt description of Barth's own modus operandi in writing this enormous book as well as its source of expansive inspiration, convoluted action, and overstated resolution. Inside the text, the metaphor embraces the competing phallocentric journals of Smith and Burlingame on one level, and the competing satires of Cooke and Barth on another. Both Smith's and Burlingame's versions of art purport to be complete histories, but each needs the other for satisfactory artistic resolution, as do Cooke's and Barth's respective *Marylandiads*. The crowning glory of Barth's recognition of the primal sexual nature of artistic competition is the magnificent conflation of his hilarious, 800-page, prize-winning novel with the great eggplant by which America was won over from its original inhabitants.

It is, however, not the phallic eggplant/art that is left hanging for the ultimate resolution, but the recipe itself: how the eggplant/art was made, or the nature of self-reflexivity in the construction of the work. Smith's original source for the recipe was the "blackamoors of Afrika" (798), perhaps the *Arabian Nights* crowd to which Barth is so indebted for his storytelling techniques. The flour paste is common; the spices, exotic and ingenious. But the ingenious construction of the artifice gives it its potential clout:

For it is the wont of men to lay hold of an Aubergine and slyce across the topp, to the end of making thinne rownd sections. But my Captain, drawing his knife from his waiste, did sever the frute into halves, splitting it lengthwise from top to bottom. Next he scor'd out a deep hollow ditch in either moietie, in such wise, but when the two halves were joyn'd like halves of an iron mould, the effect was of a deep cylindrick cavitie in the center, perhaps 3 inches in dyameter, and 7 or 8 in profunditie, for that it was an uncommon large egg-plant. (*SWF* 798–99)

Barth applies the same sort of twinning/halving twist to the construction of the novel. The bilateral philosophical arguments involving dichotomous approaches to universal questions are represented by diametrically opposed sets of characters, beginning with the Eben-Burlingame philosophies, through the bilateral debates of varying sets of opposed characters on every topic from prosodic language to the cost of a swiving, through the twinning of the historical and fictional sources already discussed and the shape-shifting double identities of most of the major characters, to the bilateral complementarity of the two versions of *The Sot-Weed Factor*, by Cooke and Barth.

There remains still a final ingredient in the recipe of transformation, the creator inserting himself into the creation:

> He next disrob'd him selfe, and before my wondering eyes lay'd hands upon his member, drawing back that part, that the Children of Israel are wont to offer to *Jehovah*, and exposing the carnall *glans*. His codd thus bar'd (wch poets have liken'd to that Serpent, that did tempt Mother Eve in the Garden), he apply'd thereto the plaister, and lay'd it within two halves of the egg-plant. There it linger'd some minutes, notwithstanding the ordeall must needs have been painfull, for all the spyce & hott things in the receipt. (799)

Here the author has magically transformed his own phallic pen together with his own history and being into something of enormous egg-plant proportion by which a bevy of Salvage Princesses, best-seller lists, markets, and fame will be taken, the mouth of the literary canon penetrated and filled to surfeit, and ultimately history made once again by the dissembling genius of artistic creation. As Barth has so often repeated, "The key to the treasure *is* the treasure."[9]

NOTES

1. In a recent study of Barth's reaction to literary predecessors, Patricia Tobin in *John Barth and the Anxiety of Continuance* (Philadelphia: University of Pennsylvania Press, 1992) convincingly applies Harold Bloom's *The Anxiety of Influence* and *A Map of Misreading* theories to Barth's works. Her definition of Bloom's thesis is particularly succinct:

> For Bloom, poetic influence since the Renaissance has been a scene of catastrophic creation, agonistic strife, and ambivalent transference, and the creativity of our strongest poets has necessarily been grounded in an antithetical and revisionary stance toward their precursors that involves negation, evasion, and extravagance. (5)

Tobin's theory is that Barth, instead of negating, joyfully seized on such an anxiety as a means of capitalizing on his literary forebears, and rather than avoiding the influences, he embraced them, revised them, and, at the same time, glorified them by going them one better. The Oedipal aspects of Bloom's thesis will be reserved for the later discussion of *Giles Goat-Boy*. For now, however, it is sufficient to note that Tobin also quite rightly claims that Barth similarly treated his own early works as part of the literary heritage upon which he drew in later works. The idea was, of course, not new with Barth, since his extensive reading of Joyce must have indicated exactly the same tendency in the earlier modernist—and so the cycle of influence on influence extends even as Barth's Möbius strip.

2. Lawrence Wroth, "*The Maryland Muse* by Ebenezer Cooke," *Proceedings of the American Antiquarian Society* 44 (October 1934): 268–78.

3. David Morrell, *John Barth: An Introduction* (University Park: Pennsylvania State University Press, 1976), pp. 33–38.

4. Leslie Fiedler, "John Barth: An Eccentric Genius," in *On Contemporary Literature*, ed. Richard Kostelanetz (New York: Avon Books, 1964), p. 240.

5. Ibid., p. 241.

6. John Enck, "John Barth: An Interview," *Wisconsin Studies in Contemporary Literature* 6 (Winter-Spring 1965): 7.

7. Charles B. Harris, *Passionate Virtuosity: The Fiction of John Barth* (Urbana: University of Illinois Press, 1983), pp. 64–65.

8. That Barth no longer stands at the recent end of the chronological line of literary succession is demonstrated by Vladimir Nabokov's magnificent *Pale Fire*, published in 1962, two years after the first publication of *Sot-Weed*. Without attempting to make a case for direct derivation, I would like to point out a few striking similarities between the two books. Both are interpretations of poems which draw their impetus from Alexander Pope. Among a number of other similarities, both books present zany versions of history. Nabokov/Kimbote's history of Zembla has sexual roots, shadowy, shape-changing figures, and a strong dose of comic homosexuality, resembling the comedy of Cooke/Barth's transformation of Maryland's history.

9. There is little doubt, at least in my mind, that Barth, even at this relatively early stage of his career—when feminist issues had yet to be fully recognized—could hardly write this male/phallocentric model of creation and artistic invention/imagination without consciously attempting a burlesque of traditional hegemony. Its ribald humor is the result of the application of excessive measures to inflict excessive potency on its excessively passive and eager female recipient. This satiric excess, extending to my interpretation of self-referentiality, rivals the proportions of Jonathan Swift's "A Modest Proposal."

4

The Revised New Syllabus: *Giles Goat-Boy*

Barth has been exceptionally explicit and candid about his ideas, structure, and methodology in writing *Giles Goat-Boy*, both in his foreword to the 1987 Anchor Doubleday edition and in a talk he gave at State University of New York–Geneseo in December 1964 (while the book was still being written) and later published as an essay in *The Friday Book*. In his comments Barth outlines his early indebtedness to Lord Raglan's *The Hero* (1936) and Joseph Campbell's *The Hero with a Thousand Faces* (1949), and also acknowledges the affinity of both *Sot-Weed* and *Giles* with Otto Rank's *Myth of the Birth of the Hero* (1914). In particular Barth is indebted to Raglan for the concept of a monomythic pattern of heroism (the idea that heroes of mythology and literature share a unified identity in that they all display similarities in origin and pursue similar courses of activity), and to Campbell for the specifics of a cyclical pattern to their actions.

The concept of every hero living through such a pattern is related to the axiom, adapted by George's teacher and surrogate parent Max Spielman, that "ontogeny [the history and development of an individual organism] recapitulates cosmogeny [the creation of the world or universe]." The application of such a law to the monomythic pattern would indicate that successive heroes through myth and literature recapitulate or experience analogous events on their way to becoming heroes. It is Barth's recital of these events in the modern terms of a mid-twentieth-century world, and, more specifically, of a fifties/sixties university campus, which provides the structure and plot of *Giles Goat-Boy*, a modern comic parody of the ancient myth-hero pattern. It also inspires one of the great comic statements in American literature.

In the plethora of critical commentary that attempted to explicate this long, dense, and surprisingly popular novel, much is made of Nietzsche, existentialism, the tragic view of the universe, and so on, but far less commentary involves the essential comic nature of the work, something my remarks will attempt to address. For now, it suffices to draw attention to Max Spielman's major contribution to learning, Spielman's Law,

> his last and farthest-reaching contribution to man's understanding of the University. That capstone on the temple of his genius, climax of his epic quest for Answers: how commonplace it sounds already, very nearly banal; and yet what dash, what vaulting insight! In three words Max Spielman synthesized all the fields which hitherto he'd browsed in brilliantly one by one—showed the "sphincter's riddle" and the mystery of the University to be the same. *Ontogeny recapitulates cosmogeny*[*sic*]—what is it but to say that proctoscopy [investigation of anal-related phenomena] repeats hagiography [biography of saints' lives]? (*G* 7)

In adhering to Spielman's Law by conducting the study of saints (i.e., heroes) in the nether regions, or the lower body poles, Barth is following the source of traditional comedy, which, as Mikhail Bakhtin so brilliantly describes it, is a product of the lower bodily functions, as opposed to the tragic and intellectual upper bodily poles.[1] Literally as well as metaphorically, Max's law is a pronouncement of Barth's examination of the monomyth, primarily through the comic lens of proctology. Even the consummate Western tragedy, *Oedipus Rex*, under a Barthean comic proctologist's lens, turns out to be basically as funny as it is gross, and both the Old and New Testaments, by which much of our culture lives, can be replaced by a Revised New Syllabus, expelled downward, like the Goat-Boy himself, from WESCAC's belly. Giles and Anastasia realize the RNS's mutually orgasmic climax in simultaneous unity with a comic universe sanctioned by WESCAC's disgorging of the postcoital couple still in their state of worldly inspired, otherworldly bliss.

The whole book is a triumph of the lower organs. Campbell's cyclical wheel (Figure 4.1) indicates a counterclockwise journey by the hero, with its climax at the lowest point, the "AXIS MUNDI," where all the really heavy learning and transfiguration go on. Both Barth and Campbell conceive of the hero's journey as a cyclical and thus recurring event, generally running counterclockwise through the cycle. A number of critical commentators have glossed in George/Giles's history such obvious attributes of the heroic pattern as his extraordinary conception and virgin birth, his murder of a rival goat, his limp, his crossing George's Gorge, his passage through Scrapegoat Grate, his sojourn in Stoker's hell, his helper-disciples, and his illumination in the coital embrace of Anastasia during a "sacred marriage" in WESCAC's belly. George does variations on his assignment not once but three times, miraculously escaping being EATen each time, and emerging

Figure 4.1
Campbell's Cyclical Wheel

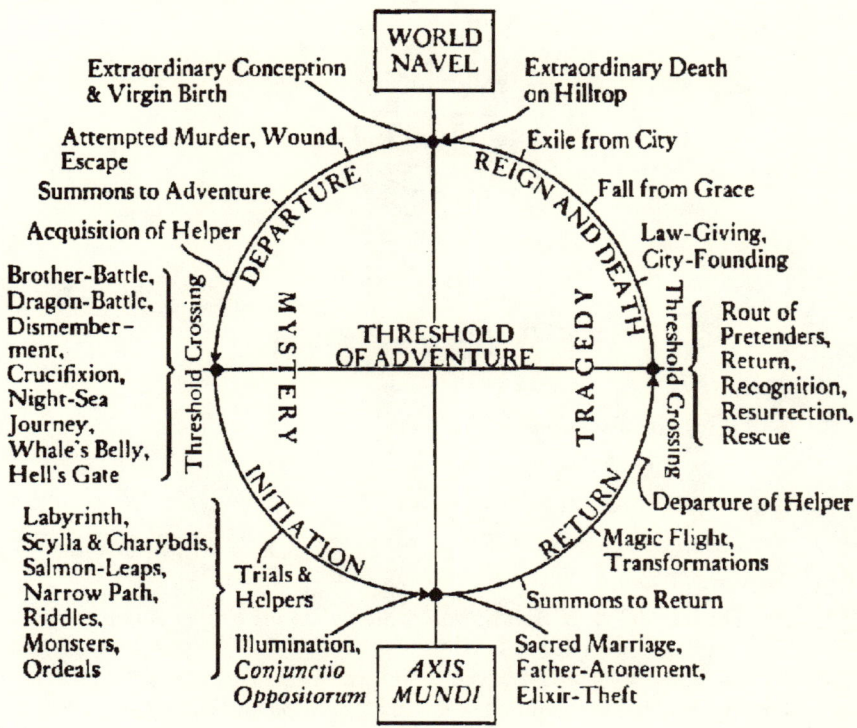

Source: John Barth, *Chimera* (New York: Random House, 1972), 261.

after each trip with a new certitude about the answers with which he survives. These ultimate answers (presumably between the relationship of right and wrong, good and bad, and what is and is not the case) are further shaded with the academic overtones of their original relation to the logo for Giles's assignment sheet (Figure 4.2). The presentation of the logo terms in the same circular context as Campbell's cyclical journey diagram implies both a serial, revolving meaning for any time/segment of the wheel and a set of oppositions that might include as well as contradict each other. The word "ALL" intervening between "PASS" and "FAIL" suggests that there is one correct or "Passed" answer, even while it suggests that all answers are correct. When each time he fulfills his assignment, Giles/George dictates his revised and successively contradictory principles to his disciples, the new philosophy and ensuing pattern of behavior demanded by the revised strictures become a source of chaos for the disciples and the campus as a whole.

Figure 4.2
Giles's Logo and Assignment Sheet

. . .

ASSIGNMENT

To Be Done At Once, In No Time

1) *Fix the Clock*
2) *End the Boundary Dispute*
3) *Overcome Your Infirmity*
4) *See Through Your Ladyship*
5) *Replace the Founder's Scroll*
6) *Pass the Finals*
7) *Present Your ID-card, Appropriately Signed, to the Proper Authority*

Source: John Barth, *Giles Boat-Boy or, The Revised New Syllabus* (Garden City, NY: Anchor/Doubleday, 1967), 383. Permission granted by Doubleday, a Division of Bantam, Doubleday, & Dell Publishing Group, Inc.

The first time around, Giles's message for the campus, and most especially for his followers or acquaintances, derives from his belief that passage is passage, and failure, failure. During the second cycle, Giles, smitten with the skepticism of seeing everything to be its opposite, preaches the sermon that passage is failure, and failure, passage. The final philosophical illumination Giles comes to and passes on to his benighted followers is that passage is both passage and failure, an all-inclusive conclusion foreshadowed by the spinning cyclical wheel on the verso of his assignment sheet.

All of Raglan's and Campbell's heroes, despite going through similar trials and events, are individuals whose own assignments are unique, universalized in only the broadest sense. Barth's own fictive stance as editorial conduit for the Revised New Syllabus casts him as both WESCAC's and Giles's surrogate who thinks of himself as going through analogous adventures. Barth assures us in his lectures and discussions on the book that this stage of his own life, the early thirties, which is the traditional midpoint of the hero's life, was one of the influences that led him to write *Giles Goat-Boy* (*G* vi). His inclusion of his own initials in the text as surrogate author/editor/plagiarist, and the doubts cast by the frame letters and posttapes on who really wrote the Revised New Syllabus and who the Grand Tutor really was all indicate that Barth, at least in some measure, identifies himself with the hero of his novel, which might be his own allegory as well as any other monomythic hero's.

Barth, in his attempt to deal with universal themes and an allegorized plot, which, by definition, is repeated over and over again throughout the history of Western civilization, asserts the timelessness of an ancient story at the same time he demonstrates its pertinence to a contemporary time frame. While various historical versions of the monomyth are always placed in a specific time and setting, the monomyth as a genre operates out of time as the repetition of a timeless cycle with no beginning or end. Certainly two of the most fertile settings for the comic parodist are the mid-twentieth century of *Giles* and *The Sot-Weed Factor*'s eighteenth-century setting, for the two periods, with their contradictory rationalizations for contemporary cultural behavior and the chaotic pace of their intellectual discovery, provide an aptly satiric cultural lens to view the universal proceedings of a monomyth with popular versions frozen in earlier Greek, Roman, or Christian periods.

While the whole of *Giles Goat-Boy* consists of comic time warps of the ancient myth made modern, Barth's most blatant and comical parody is his updated version of *Oedipus Rex*, relocated to a university campus, offered in its ribald entirety to the West Campus audience, and recapitulated in the novel as a whole by the hero, George, the Goat-Boy, in his innocent lust for Lady Cream Hair, his own mother. Giles shares other monomythic heroic attributes with Oedipus/Taliped, such as their origins, limps, and truth-seeking introspection. But the essential comic connection is the riddle of the sphinx/sphincters. Just as every man walks successively on four, two, and three legs, so, as we have already noted, do the sphincters in Spielman's Law dictate a comic cycle oriented to the lower bodily pole depicted in *Giles*.

The play also draws our attention to Giles as a combination of the two monomythic figures, Christ and Oedipus. Giles, like Oedipus, engages in serious mistakes in a genuine quest for self-knowledge, while at the same time, like Christ, he constantly sees his revelations as being wholly correct, since they come from the Grand Tutor himself. It's the same sort of comic-identity-Catch-22 Joyce exploits in "Grace," where, according to the comforters' account, the Pope declared himself infallible by reason of his own papal infallibility. Revelation is a sort of divine comedy, Barth suggests, as well as the low side of human tragedy.

The *Oedipus Rex* parody is one extended bawdy joke, with Dean Taliped's (Oedipus's) mother/wife as an aging outspoken nymphomaniac offering herself to nearly everybody, including the mailman. Capitalizing on the comic aspects of Freud's serious interpretation of the play, Barth reduces Taliped to childish drivel in his conversations with his mother, and turns Gynander's (Tiresias's) hermaphroditic wisdom into the epithets of a homosexual queen. Gynander's name implies a meandering gynocentrism which mixes the sexes as the object of a sort of redneck sophomoric joke to complement the same sort of humor Barth develops in the Oedipal situation where mother-as-sex-symbol becomes the comic figure objectifying the seamy impulses of the serious. Barth as a consummate comic artist thus explores aspects of the tragedy that are undeniable if normally unmentionable. Freud's universalization of mother-love and the dark side of the subconscious makes lechers of us all, desacralizing our shibboleths even as did Campbell and Raglan in their inclusion of a traditional deity in the monomyth cycle, and thus rendering the whole business a potential traffic for the satirist and the clown. When Agenora insists that Taliped tell her "I WUV OO VEWWY MUCH" (*G* 285), she comically takes a lot of the tragic dread out of the infantilized human condition.

Updated slang and metaphors complement the new low meanings put on everything in the play. The chorus, consisting of ever-political department chairs, address their dean in choruses of limericks, accentuating further Barth's tendency toward multisyllabic rhyme and ingenious internal rhyme producing unexpected syntactically nutty sentences which run into succeeding lines where full stops would have been the norm. The sophomoric ingeniousness of the comic inversions is worthy of Barth's image of knowledge seekers as adolescents, when, as Max tells us, "*Self-knowledge . . . is always bad news*" (*G* 85).

While Barth treats the tragic view of life adopted by the Western world, exemplified by a monomythic hero whose chief end in life lies in the Socratic tradition of knowing himself at any cost, Barth also comically engages the religiosity associated with the monomyth, in which the hero is himself a divinity. While Oedipus attaches himself to the extra-natural forces that rule the universe by solving the riddle of the sphinx—an answer in which the cyclical life pattern of man provides the ultimate solution—he operates always inside human boundaries, subject to all the fate, foibles, and hubris that are the lot of the species. On the other hand, the divinity of a God situated temporarily in a man's body provides us with a second, supernatural, version of the heroic monomyth, in which the God as scapegoat figure suffers a personal atonement for humanity in order to satisfy the demands of an even more powerful Godlike figure. In retrospect, the Campbell-Raglan monomyth thesis casts some doubt on the divinity of such heroes as Christ, who follow the path of the hero, but whose belief in their own divinity is constantly challenged by the very skeptical people the heroes are trying to save. The ur-myth itself occupies some middle ground between traditional fiction and a recognizable pattern in the lives of all people, like nature itself, common enough to assume the stature either of a divine and purposeful plan, or a manifestation of perpetual meaninglessness with its resulting chaos. It is this choice that Barth seizes on to exemplify in *Giles Goat-Boy*.

Enos Enoch, the Christ surrogate in the novel and the ultimate Grand Tutor, operates as the original Western intermediary between the Founder or originator of the campus-universe and its student citizens. The existence of the primordial deity is never brought into serious, that is, comic, question. But the evolving tradition out of which the Son came certainly is. How does a potential Grand Tutor know that he is in fact destined to be (or is) a Grand Tutor? Is he foolish? a charlatan? self-deluded? In the normal mythic herohood of Aeneas, Dante, and the others, predestination is only an issue insofar as they are all convinced that they, as mortals, are only the human instruments of some fatalistic or Godlike power who has chosen them to found Rome, or to glimpse and reveal the afterlife. It is a lousy job, but somebody has to do it.

Barth chose for his protagonist an innocent whose certainty of his own divinity was tenuous at best, sometimes firm, sometimes denied, a naïf who was always fallible, with more wrong answers than right, and someone without the traditional Christian patriarchal trappings of celibacy, serenity, and unblemished wisdom. Barth combined the ends of holy or theocentric herohood with humanistic herohood by exploiting the paradoxes that arise between tradition and contemporary reality, paradoxes that are best developed through comic inversions where the inherent contradictions form satiric correctives to the perversions of reality committed by traditional religious dogmas. In the process Barth's comic vision employed excess in the same way that burlesque often does. *Giles* is not simply satiric, as is the classical satire of Jonathan Swift; but rather burlesque in the tradition of the old Saturnalia or carnivalesque, in which the comic inverts traditional social and historical tenets and exposes their low comic counterparts. The emphasis on lenses and corrections and distortions of real events, which manifest themselves in Giles's walking-stick/divining-rod, is the very comic corrective that leads eventually to his understanding of difference and ultimately the sameness of the apparently contradictory. The learning process represented in the hero's journey is aptly characterized as a grand continuing tour through a university campus (the name *university* implying all of the known universe). The academic, curricular aspects of the hero's journey through undergraduate life provide Barth with the potential to include all of human knowledge and at the same time afford a modern variation on the tradition of the heroic monomyth.

The late fifties and early sixties setting of the novel is contemporaneous with the time of the book's composition, and affected readers' responses to the book. Part of the enormous popularity *Giles* enjoyed was drawn from the aptness of the campus-in-chaos metaphor. During the sixties with its love-ins, "happenings," general protests, and major reexamination of tradition and propagandistic history, the proximity of the setting to the immediate campus time frame meant that most of the historical counterparts of the *Giles* characters and events were fairly understandable to most students reading the book for the first time. Without having to think too much or work too hard, readers found they could participate in Barth's allusion game and to a certain extent understand the metaphoric content of much of the book, even without going to the library or class lectures. *Giles* gave many such readers their first opportunity at personal identification with an erudite work of contemporary fiction. The conditions that led to *Giles*'s popularity among those readers are fast fading, as the experiences of the post–World War II generation have been lost to the aspiring yuppies of the nineties. Even so, most students are still able to identify a cataclysm like the Second Riot as the Second World War, and associate the Seigfrieders with Germans, the Student Unionists with communists, the EAT with the nuclear button, the various sections of the university with different blocs of countries, and the campus dividing line with the Iron Curtain/Berlin Wall between Eastern and Western bloc nations. The Jewish holocaust and the political tensions that every day threatened to break out in world destruction, while dimming in the minds of today's sophomores, remain vaguely identifiable by the present generation, even if not the next. But with the length of the book inhibiting the casual reader and the immediacy of the recognition factor fading, the market has shrunk to a few stalwarts keeping despair alive by requiring the text in their contemporary literature courses.

The tendency to identify *Giles*'s characters with specific historical individuals, while it has some immediate gratification, can also be misleading; besides having some historical counterpart, most of Barth's characters are also generic types, not quite mythic, but certainly typical of those who hold various philosophical, political, historical, and psychological positions. The characters are so given over to stereotypical behavior that Barth has often been accused of creating unreal people, or characters without individualizing personal humanity. For example, Eblis Eierkopf is a Wernher von Braun figure in his insistence on science, his penchant for Teutonic accuracy, and his understanding of physics, but he is also a quintessential egghead on a literal as well as a metaphorical level; and Max Spielman, with his scientific theorizing and socialist leanings—racked over the enormity of the EAT machine he created, and drummed off campus—certainly resembles Robert Oppenheimer, but also is a suffering servant, a brilliant practical philosopher, and a prototypical Jewish caricature. The Living Sakhyan is not unlike the Dalai Lama, but also represents Eastern mysticism and worldly detachment in general. Even the characters most easily identifiable with single figures, the Rexfords with John and Jackie Kennedy, operate within their own pragmatic context and derive personal popularity from America's national Camelot myth rather than from decisive or idealistic action on behalf of the campus they govern.

The characters who interact with Giles the most are also the most fully described. In addition, they tend to be psychologically intertwined with broader national and international psyches and issues and, ultimately, with human values. Anastasia, George's Ladyship, is, on the personal level, his major supporter, lover, and tutor-in-climax, while at the same time she is the consummate female victim, suffering/enjoying the bestial lusts of the whole campus seriatim. She has the overtones of Tolstoy's Anastasia, as a constant source of inspiration, but one which is localized in her crotch, the metaphor which inspires, as it ultimately does with Giles, or destroys, as it does with G. Herrold. Giles's perplexing assignment of getting to know her is never convincingly fulfilled in all of its implications. His remarkably detailed physical examination of her, complemented by his coital/mystical examination and achievement of some spiritual nirvana in the ecstasy of orgasmic knowledge, yields a mystical, undefinable peace in love, but one that is only transitory, except in memory. In many respects Barth's failure to define her except as caricature is appropriate to this novel of burlesque, since all characters are in a sense represented as metaphors. This tendency is less apparent in the other characters because the reader is less apt to feel pity and fear for their situation. Anastasia's is such that some of her innocent suffering, like that of Nabokov's Lolita, draws us beyond the protagonist's distorted consciousness, to a pity and fear identified with common humanity that militates against burlesque intent.

Anastasia's vulva, the "dark beacon of George's Gorge," is reminiscent of the green light at the end of Daisy's dock that had summoned Gatsby to his ruinous fate, while Anastasia's relieving so many others of their sexual anxieties lies somewhere between wantonness and martyrdom, as Barth in character after character plays off sophomoric, rednecked stereotypes that in the new lens of the nineties seem more offensive than they first did. For instance, the representation of Croaker as absolute, barely controllable primitive, swiving his way across campus, is far more offensive now than in the early sixties when Barth wrote the book. But, on the other hand, the quintessential American, Peter Greene, with his tortured schizoid self-loathing and self-assurance, and his affinity for stereotypes, especially in his rationalizations for his own miscegenation with G. Herrold's daughter, certainly seems to embody national truths as timely now as they were in 1965 or in the days of Huckleberry Finn.

Max, Leonid, and Comrade X all join Greene in representing variations on human preoccupation with suffering and guilt in all their culturally and socially related permutations. Sear, a more complex intellectual figure because he has already vicariously experienced so much through his immense erudition and his voyeuristic vocation as psychiatrist, is a traditional, jaded, campus-intellectual pervert constantly seeking new thrills to tickle his cerebrum as well as his genitalia, in contrast with the innocents, Giles, Greene, and Leonid. Sear, whose sexual practices and experiments are as various as his knowledge, is the Tiresias figure of the campus. His knowledge of the past, especially Sophocles, is formidable, and his predictions of the human condition are just as tragic as Oedipus's seminal search for self-knowledge. However, his reading and fluoroscope lens define the limits of his exploration of the human condition, since, like Giles, he doesn't seem to understand the concept of love. His explanation of the goals of his marriage—"it's the only *authentic* and *meaningful* kind of marriage, for educated people in modern terms, because it's based on freedom, frankness, equality, and no illusions whatever" (*G* 473)—sounds like it might have come from the whacked out intelligence of Joe Morgan in *The End of the Road*.

Barth gets a great deal of mileage out of pairing such stereotypically opposite characters as the rival brothers Lucius (light)—the quintessential leader for human (campus) improvement and peace—with Maurice (dark)—the force of chaos. Barth also pairs Eierkopf's debilitating mechanistic technical genius with Croaker's mindless vitality. It is the combination of the severally deficient characters that provides a means of rudimentary survival for the couples, and their collective interaction that speaks to the all-inclusive final answers to the final test of acceptability for commencement.

The most problematical pair of characters is Giles and Bray. Occasionally reminiscent of Eben and Burlingame in *Sot-Weed*, their natures are respectively naïve and jaded, innocent and cunning, pretentious and false. We never find out whether Bray is merely a clever charlatan or a real grand tutor, or, for that matter, whether Giles is a deluded overachiever or a divinely destined superhero. Bray does exhibit some of the same characteristics as Giles, in that they are both pretenders to a divinely inspired or computer-sanctioned leadership role. Bray may be in many ways the dark subconscious of Giles, a yang to his yin. But in any event they participate in the same rivalries for divinity as do Rexford and Stoker for popular leadership. This recurrent alter-ego relationship may also play a role in announcing Barth's own divided psyche and in the reflexive aspect of his works in general. John Tilton traces Bray's origins to an early Maryland Anglican clergyman who bestowed false absolutions on all, an evangelical leader representing "institutionalized religion," and thus an agent for evil in Tilton's clear-cut distinction between good and bad.[2] Tilton is one of many critics who see Giles's ultimate assignment as reconciliation or blending of opposites, or the thesis and antithesis of the Hegelian dialectic in one harmonious and all-inclusive synthesis.[3] This explanation would tend to be borne out by Giles and Anastasia simultaneously pushing the buttons for both contradictory answers in WESCAC's final examination, and Giles's decision that everything is both itself and its opposite in his final round of messages to his disciples. At the same time, everything meaning everything conversely implies that nothing has any meaning when all and nothing are equivalents. The entire all-inclusive proposition makes the Living Sakhyan's aloof approach to the problem even more realistic in its denial of meaning or the importance of specifics.

If Barth's characters represent a panoply of opposing archetypal approaches to life against a background of contemporary history, this does not mean that he has neglected the enormous body of Western literature upon which he drew so heavily in *Sot-Weed*. *The Divine Comedy*, already an example of the theocentric approach to the monomythic pattern, provides fertile material for allusion in *Giles Goat-Boy*. Stoker's power house is another inferno, as is Main Detention, with its graduated levels of sinners and individual appropriate punishments. What Barth emphasizes, and what Dante, in his piety, missed, is that the power—that is, vitality—of life (and, incidentally, Dante's own pious poem) is driven by power house types. Stoker, a Mephistopheles figure, also doubles as a Virgil to Giles's innocent Dante figure (whose only crime seems to have been lust), while Giles, ignorant of the traditional strictures on the carnal, celebrates and lives the simple drives of nature. Through a succession of dates connected with the seasons of the year and particularly the role of the solstices, the carnivalesque power house party culminates in the burial of the dead (G. Herrold) and the metaphoric rebirth of life in the form of the climactic celebration of Giles's coming of age during his first servicing of Anastasia. Stoker, a leathercoated version of Marlon Brando in *The Wild One*, has Brando's dark vision of power and a sense of morality which precludes tradition. The carnival/party in the power house is as full of primitive energy, celebration, and exuberance as its leader. Stoker seems to be charged himself with the vital power he provides to the campus in his role as antagonist to established power. Founder's Hill, with its ever-standing shaft, is at the other end of the power spectrum, but tied to the cycle with phallic immediacy.

Chicky's hippie lover is the real if inadvertent prophet of the book and, for that matter, the rest of the Barth canon, when the lover leads Giles to suppose that *Being* is copulating, and that copulating is what life is all about. Sex, the Key to the Treasure (What's in a phallic phrase?), marks the beginning and end of Giles's education about the nature of life. The solstices that inspired ur-religious worship have their origins in the reproductive cycle, and thus in life itself, and the carnivalistic celebrations that complement and defy traditional religious practices are the innate human response to the mysteries of life rendered in terms of the natural.

Putting a whole new twist on Hamlet's "To be or not to be . . . ," Anastasia fulfills the role of every stereotypical life-giver, allowing Giles to pass through WESCAC's innards in a state of heavenly bliss, in full physical consummation that rises to the level of mysticism in their love. We are first introduced to Anastasia as she suffers the thrusts of Croaker, whose gift of primitive carnal vitality is conveyed in ancient indecipherable carvings on Giles's stick (another phallic metaphor) with a beauty and majesty that apparently belie their source, but in fact are part of the vitality they represent. Sex is the common thread tying all of the characters of *Giles Goat-Boy* and the rest of Barth's books together, and certainly the motivating force of most of the characters. What Rabelais did in glorification of wine, Barth exceeds in his sexual devotion.

Croaker's carved legacy is but one of three testaments by which, as in all Barth's books, the deeds of heroes and ordinary men are made known. The record/story/history/creative product/explanation itself is always the centerpiece of each work. And in *Giles* it is compared to the sacred texts of the Judeo-Christian world. We are invited to entertain the idea that the computer tapes from which the text of the book is purportedly set are the Revised New Testament, an account of Giles's life, just as the New Testament is an account of Christ's. Both documents are of doubtful authorship; both have their challengers; both have been worked over, rearranged, and revised by scholars; and both have generated their own disciples—all with their own variations and interpretations of the stories, as we learn from the posttapes. By replacing the scrolls with his own history, the Revised New Syllabus, Giles has given campus scholars and hagiographers a whole modern realm of data to draw upon for their reformulation of the monomyth. What WESCAC needed was a saint/subject in its own era, a product of its own microchips, even if the spermatozoa came from a distillation of worthy undergraduate prostates. It is no accident that the new word made flesh came out of the library, since all books and records have their eternal homes there. The computer is a twentieth-century invention producing a twentieth-century God born of a virgin librarian in the depths of the stacks and tape storage rooms. The history and the composition of the new Grand Tutor's life embodied in the tapes constitutes a contemporary hagiography of the lower comic order, a proctoscopy of bizarre, cyclical, comic events upon which the universe is founded and driven, the entire enterprise related in the pattern of the heroic monomyth. It is not entirely out of the realm of possibility that in another 2,000 years biblical scholars coming upon *Giles Goat-Boy* in the ruins might eventually derive the same basic message out of it that present hagiographers glean from our own ancient sources.

In the broadest possible sense, with the Revised New Syllabus, Barth/Giles has indeed replaced the Founder's Scroll—the product, even as is this commentary, of a computer. WESCAC is, in effect, God, impregnating a virgin, slaughtering thousands, responsible for its own history, the silent, awesome power that pervades our campus-world as it did the Judaic tradition. While it is comforting to know that the computer is only a man-created machine, it is not one we would with an easy mind pull the plug on, since the ultimate repercussions are unpredictable. The enormity of creating a new Bible out of the whole universe of past history and contemporary existence is, if nothing else, a venture exceeding in chutzpa even books about an immigrant soldier's founding Rome or a living traveler's touring the afterlife.

The questions raised by the frame paraphernalia (the Publisher's Disclaimer, J.B.'s Cover Letter to the Editors and Publisher, the Posttape, the Postscript to the Posttape, and the Footnote to the Postscript to the Posttape) introduce Barth or a fictive author with the initials J.B. into the text of the book, if not the narrative itself. The frame material elaborates and raises questions regarding authenticity and authorial intent. Prefatory matter includes the reactions of the several editors, who give preview versions of critical reaction to the book. While the diversity of the four editors' opinions covers a spectrum of reaction, mostly negative, to the book, it reminds the reader of Swift's similar artifice in *Gulliver's Travels*.

Even though the original draft of the book is supposed to have been in the form of a computer tape, what the mysterious visitor deposits on J.B.'s desk is a typescript. Stoker Giles delivers to J.B. the New Revised Syllabus compiled by WESCAC from old files and all the accounts and information the computer could muster, using J.B. as a conduit to the publishers. J.B.'s position is similar to John Barth's at the time. J.B. had already started and stalled his creative motor on a similar book, entitled *The Seeker*, and is reminded by Stoker Giles that his proposed hero has a number of correspondences to the monomythic hero, much in the way that Barth was reminded that Ebeneezer Cooke and Henry Burlingame bore similar resemblances to the prototype. The book J.B. admits to be working on might easily become *Giles Goat-Boy*. Moreover, the protagonist of J.B.'s putative book "would deal with reality like a book, a novel that he didn't write and wasn't a character in, but only an appreciative reader of. . . . But in truth, of course, he *wasn't* finally a spectator at all: he couldn't stay 'out of it' " (*G* xxv), a situation exactly like J.B.'s relation to *Giles*. Furthermore, the author as self-reflexive monomythic hero-seeker is always included in his own monomythic stories, appearing in fictional versions of his own life, just as the Revised New Syllabus is a new creative version of the Founder's Scroll/ur-Bible. Stoker's reply to J.B.'s idea of authorial involvement in the text indicates that J.B. has the wrong idea, and the concept of such self-reflexivity is a kind of hoax, just as Bray's Grand-Tutorial bid is little more than an ingeniously clever hoax. Even though in *Giles* Bray never claimed to write his own Revised New Syllabus, he came back in *LETTERS* to do just that, with the aid of a miraculous computer and sacrificial women, all of whom he may or may not have impregnated.

Beverly Gross, in her negative response to *Giles*, accuses Barth himself of being a Bray figure, a copycat, and a clever charlatan excreting a slippery ooze:

That slippery ooze, remember, is the last trace of the vanishing Harold Bray, professed Grand Tutor and champion impostor. In fact, if there is a single character who seems most to capture the spirit of the author in Barth's works it is probably this same Harold Bray: omniscient, omnipresent, a man of many masks but no face, a false prophet, perhaps a true genius. But who is to know?[4]

Gross missed the point of the book: Passed and Flunked are interchangeable, one and the same thing. Barth is both a Giles and a Bray, writing the book of himself and at the same time making an ingenious hoax of the whole enterprise. Not only is Barth revealing both sides of himself, but in so doing, he is following in the very footsteps of his literary forebears. To underscore and at the same time obfuscate the murky duality of the book's major proposition and authorship, Barth's post-matter calls into question the identity and roles of Stoker Giles, J.B., and WESCAC, as well as the authenticity of both the Revised New Syllabus and its origins. Why not? We have had a grand time, and Barth will devote his entire next book to exploring the funhouse labyrinth of self-reflexivity.

NOTES

1. Mikhail Bakhtin, *Rabelais and His World*, trans. Helene Iswolsky (Cambridge, Mass.: MIT Press, 1968), p. 21.

2. John W. Tilton, "*Giles Goat-Boy*: An Interpretation," *Bucknell Review* 18, no. 1 (1970): 98–100.

3. Charles B. Harris (*Passionate Virtuosity: The Fiction of John Barth* [Urbana: University of Illinois Press, 1983]), Jac Tharpe (*John Barth: The Comic Sublimity of Paradox* [Carbondale: Southern Illinois University Press, 1974]), and Stan Fogel and Gordon Slethaug (*Understanding John Barth* [Columbia: University of South Carolina Press, 1990]) are but three of many who see the reconciliation/synthesis theme as the point of the book. Harris (87–88) also cites Peter Mercer, John Tilton, Stanley Fish, and Robert Scholes as drawing similar conclusions.

4. Beverly Gross, "The Anti-Novels of John Barth," *Chicago Review* 20, no. 3 (November 1968): 95.

5

Funhouse Reflexes:
Lost in the Funhouse

Lost in the Funhouse has a lot of James Joyce in it. Jan Marta, among others, has long recognized the self-referentiality in the two halves of the book as resembling both the *Küntstlerroman* and *Bildungsroman* prototypes of *Portrait*.[1] However, Barth's volume of short stories and Joyce's *Dubliners* also bear striking resemblances. Like *Dubliners*, *Funhouse* is, according to Barth,

> a *book* of short stories: a sequence or series rather than a mere assortment . . . strung . . . together on a few echoed and developed themes and . . . circl[ing] . . . back upon itself: not to close a simple circuit like that of Joyce's *Finnegans Wake*, emblematic of Viconian eternal return, but to make a circuit with a twist to it, like a Möbius strip. (*F* vii)

When Gabriel Conroy composes the concluding words of *Dubliners* in "The Dead," he forges a Möbius connection of living and dead by juxtaposing the final Christlike (and hence resurrectable) image of Michael Furey against that of the dying priest in the opening story, "The Sisters." Father Flynn's ideas of the world seemed so lunatic that they "made them think that there was something gone wrong with him."[2] Fat May, who sits outside the funhouse, laughing inexplicably at nothing, complements the image of the priest sitting, laughing inexplicably, in the confessional.

Both books begin with a series of first-person narrations of young people, a series of loosely associated *Bildungsroman* experiences, later broadened into the personal experiences of increasingly older characters, and finally into a study of institutions, before returning to a writer-centered focus on the death-life cycle. Joyce was not to address openly the process of making self-conscious fiction until *Ulysses*, but it is a topic that structurally and thematically permeates his *Künstlerroman*, *A Portrait of the Artist as a Young Man*, a story so self-conscious it might have been written by the Minstrel of "Anonymiad."[3] Our final glimpse of Stephen Dedalus's literary artistry is his diary, committed to posterity amidst a combination of hysterically joyous and despairing platitudes.

The great difference between *Funhouse* and Joyce's first two volumes of fiction is that Barth's statement of self-conscious intent is openly made, even trumpeted, with all the self-reflexive difficulties of its composition blatantly and painstakingly examined. His narratives always obviously work inward to their own composition rather than outward, like Joyce's, to the description of a world separate from as well as a part of their author, who ultimately pretends to stand by, "indifferent, paring his fingernails," even while we see him in the agony of squeezing a villanelle out of his own humiliations and feelings of sexual impotence.

The concluding diary entries of *Portrait* recapitulate the introductory overture of sight and sound images filtered through Stephen Dedalus's early childhood perception, which begins the book, implying that he will eventually write the novel of his discovery of the means and subject matter for his narcissistic representation of himself. Barth follows the same idea with an author-character living a fiction of his own devising, a motif that permeates *Lost in the Funhouse*. All the *Portrait* activities, like those of the *Funhouse* stories, are those that Stephen participated in and transformed into the artistic consciousness that narrates the novel. In a sense *Portrait* and *Funhouse* both use variations on the protagonist/narrator technique of Gabriel Conroy's conclusion of *Dubliners*.

As Charles Harris tells us, Ambrose is really the "narrator/protagonist of *Lost in the Funhouse*."[4] As is the case with *Dubliners*, Ambrose appears in three chronological accounts of his youth. His doppelgänger appears in intervening stories, which are projections of events and attitudes in the Ambrose narratives, and, as he becomes distanced in time and more overwhelmed by the problems of composition, we can see him identified with the self-conscious author-narrators of the later stories. Andrea and Magda of the Ambrose stories evolve into ur-heroines for the rest of the fiction, while Peter, Ambrose's brother, becomes an archetypical sibling rival, and the problem of self-identity is transformed into a metaphor for the problems of creating self-conscious fiction. In this last respect, then, *Lost in the Funhouse* becomes for Barth what *Dubliners* and *Portrait* were for Joyce.

The above character transformations, eventually depicted metaphorically in Proteus's identity changes in "Menelaiad," are circumscribed by the

Möbius strip, which structurally embodies the "Frame-Tale" and thus the rest of the book. The water messages that Ambrose finds are his fictionalized and metaphorized links to the stories themselves, really about his and the minstrel/surrogate's love affairs and devotion to the sterilities and problems of creating fiction, or funhouses for others, as Ambrose tells us in "Lost in the Funhouse" and reiterates halfway through, in "Title." Following the path of the Möbius strip, the reader returns not once but many times to the beginning, made strange by the reader's facing a direction opposite to the one he did on the previous trip. In the final circle, at least one of the jars set adrift in "Anonymiad" returns in "Night-Sea Journey" as the self-conscious primal progress of the existential sperm, who presumably is to become Ambrose in the next story. By draining, then "humping" the jar before loading it with his manuscript and setting it adrift on the sea, the minstrel/author/self-creator, Ambrose, has committed the ultimate self-reflexivity, in "authoring" himself both as writer and seedbearer. The doubt-riddled, existential sperm begins his journey through self-narration, passing himself many times, always in angst, in identity and creativity crises, driven by primal forces to a sexual union in which the self is obliterated, singing "Love! Love! Love!" just as the boy in Joyce's "Araby" murmurs "O love!, O love! many times," as they both press onward toward the unknown they are forced to define in some sort of ultimate epiphanic fiction.

Hector Mensch, the husband of Ambrose's mother, in keeping with the notion of self-generation, had such doubts about the boy's parentage that he was driven into an insane asylum, and Andrea, Ambrose's mother, is described as beautiful and sensual, a ripe object for Oedipal affection, and an inspiration for Ambrose's later version of Helen and her relations with the gullible storyteller Menelaus. The story "Ambrose His Mark," while realistic, is narrated from baby Ambrose's point of view by an older Ambrose who refers in passing to events that won't happen for years after the story's present.

The second Ambrose story, "Water-Message," takes place when he is in the fourth grade, and depicts him as a creative if increasingly solitary youngster. The mature third-person narration is free of the self-consciousness of the emerging pubescent narrator of the third story, "Lost in the Funhouse." Thus the chronological maturity of the narrators of the early stories runs contrary to the age of their protagonist, even though narrator and protagonist are ultimately the same. In "Water-Message" Ambrose concocts a wish-fulfillment story of a romantic relationship with Peggy Robbins, whose romantic escapades had earlier been darkly hinted by the older boys accompanying his brother. Ambrose's tale, which makes him the recipient of her favors, immediately precedes his finding a blank message in a bottle, addressed "TO WHOM IT MAY CONCERN," and signed merely, "YOURS TRULY." Once Ambrose has seen the message, its blank character invites him to fill in the mystery for himself, to supply the composition, to provide the fun for the fictive lovers rather than to be a lover himself. His life will be in a sense vicarious, and can become any reality his fictive mind can make it. The whole foreshadows the similar epiphany Ambrose extracts from his later funhouse adventure, all confirming the mark of the tale-teller, St. Ambrose, whose name he has inherited. In this naturalistic fiction, or fictive creation-represented-as-truth, Ambrose bears the name and sign of the elocutionist, the storyteller, who is destined to fill in the blanks of his own water message. They will stem in part from his own experience and in part from his libidinous, literary, and romantic projections of the meaning of that existence.

Two other tales interrupt the continuing autobiographical account of Ambrose's childhood: "Autobiography: A Self-Recorded Fiction" and "Petition." Both deal with the problems proposed by Ambrose's discoveries. The first was presented by Barth at guest readings as a tape to which he both intermittently listened and retired from the stage. In it the self represented in fiction stands disembodied: a voice crippled by the vagaries and distortions of its author, conceived from the Author/father's background out of penless expediency. Neither self-fulfilling nor true, nor artistically endowed with the stuff of greatness, it becomes a soul in a sort of media limbo contributing to its own being, presumably suggesting courses for its own activities, but incapable of drawing to its own conclusion—the beginning of Ambrose's problems as a self-conscious writer.

"Petition," Barth's first attempt at the epistolary form, involves a sort of ingenuous, if primitive, Freudian approach to Ambrose's problems with his brother. Imposing Barth himself as a biographical prototype of Ambrose creates a number of problems, especially with chronology. If Ambrose were roughly Barth's own age (his pubescent voice was breaking about 1943–44), the petition, dated April 21, 1931, would have been written by an Ambrose a little less than a year old. Scholars have pointed out the actual visit to the United States of a dignitary reminiscent of Majesty Prajadhipok in 1931,[5] so an older Ambrose would have to do a little research to give historical credence to his Siamese twin conceit. The narrator is mature enough to have envisioned the physical complications of a back-to-front arrangement with regard to defecating, lovemaking, and so on, and used them to his advantage in the letter writer's depiction of himself as practically without smell, and with little potency other than that of the imagination. Certainly such a comparison between brothers—one crude, licentious, and physically self-gratifying, the other deprived of freedom in his brother's shadow, spiritual, introverted, literary, and self-pitying—is a reflection of Ambrose's scarcely repressed feelings in his sibling situation with Peter, the sexual jealousy played out against the hilarious backdrop of the inescapable subservience of the smaller brother's position in life. The dilemma of authorial involvement has, as we will repeatedly see in Barth, its comic side.

Yet in "Petition" the obvious authorial involvement never becomes an open reflexivity; there are no authorial comments on composition, and the whole piece is written as if the conceit of the twins were a fact of fictive existence. The story thus becomes doubly satiric in the extent to which an author (Ambrose) can be psychologically involved in his story about a narrator (the letter writer) pretending to neutrality, while at the same time the schizophrenic psychology behind the twin's exercise in scriptotherapy is readily apparent. The anguished creativity of the petitioner is that of the petitioner's creator, Ambrose. Barth playfully leaves open the question of whether Ambrose's angst similarly mirrors his creator's. The story forms a fitting introduction to the fraternal rivalry of the two autobiographical Ambrose stories that surround it, so that we are led to question where self-conscious fiction leaves off and traditional narrative begins.

In most of the criticism of "Lost in the Funhouse," little is made of the naïve character of the authorial intrusions, especially in the first few pages of the story. First, the narration is laced with the eighteenth-century affectation of dates, names, and places composed partially with dashes ("19_____," "B_____ Street" "D_____, Maryland," "Magda G_____," etc.) as if some delicately prudent sensibility dictated that reality be humanely obscured by the author, whose real reason was to imply verisimilitude through the device. Also in the first few pages we are struck by admonitions about technique that one might easily find in an elementary creative writing text, coupled with other naïve bits of freshman erudition ("as mentioned in the novel *The 42nd Parallel* by John Dos Passos . . .," or, "The Irish author James Joyce, in his unusual novel entitled *Ulysses*, now available in this country, uses the adjectives *snot-green* and *scrotum tightening* to describe the sea" [*F* 73–74]). All of these things point to an early attempt by an adolescent author. Yet "Lost in the Funhouse," youthful and error-filled as it may appear, becomes the most discussed story in the collection, with ultimately emerging meanings about the structure and plot line of the whole book. The narrative remains shrouded in intriguing ambiguity, even if on the surface it appears totally accessible. A blatant self-consciousness is increasingly apparent, as the very writing of the story promotes more and more sophisticated narrative anguish about composition in addition to the emerging *Küntslerroman* lessons of the situation to

Ambrose. The story is about its own compositional maturation as well as Ambrose's personal epiphanies regarding his place in life and the fiction he will write, and, indeed, is writing. Throughout there are sentences broken off as if thoughts were either abandoned or so obvious in their conclusion that they did not have to be written, and interruptions in which the authorial intrusion becomes part of a quote on which it is commenting:

"I warn you, I've never been through it before," he added, *laughing easily*; "but I reckon we can manage somehow. The important thing to remember, after all, is that it's meant to be a *fun*house; that is a place of amusement. If people really get lost or injured or too badly frightened in it, their owner'd go out of business. There'd even be law suits. No character in a work of fiction can make a speech this long without interruption or acknowledgment from the other characters."(*F* 90)

Barth's donnée is that Ambrose sees himself as a character in a fiction even as he is participating in "real" acts that in Ambrose's perception become fictional metaphors. Thus, the reader is given a window on Ambrose's creative cogitations even as he translates external action into fiction. Ambrose's story is represented as an artistic recreation of his experiences while they happen, a snapshot in time already distorted by hindsight and distance. Even though Barth seeds the story with first-draft mistakes and out-of-place guidelines to make the creation seem spontaneous, we can only assume that Ambrose had to have written it at a later point in time. The sequence is tantalizingly close to what Ambrose's creative father, Barth, gives us in the development of his own compositional theories through the Ambrose fiction. In his introduction to the Anchor Books edition of *Funhouse*, Barth tells us that Ambrose's visit to Ocean City, Maryland, had only a rough counterpart in Barth's youth to a visit to Asbury Park (*F* viii). The rest is an Ambrose-like self-conscious embellishment.

Oddly enough, the concluding paragraph of this complex artifice is apparently intended as a traditional revelation of truth for its protagonist and the faithful reader, a cornerstone of fictive bedrock which will explain style, meaning, structure, and the rest:

He wishes he had never entered the funhouse. But he has. Then he wishes he were dead. But he's not. Therefore he will construct funhouses for others and be their secret operator—though he would rather be among the lovers for whom funhouses are designed. (*F* 97)

Most critics take this at face value, but with Barth that's dangerous. Certainly the statement is Ambrose talking about himself, trying at his neophyte stage to give a traditionally satisfying conclusion to the story. The

Byronesque romantic desperation of the outcast artist represents the same sort of naïveté Stephen Dedalus conveyed in the conclusion of *Portrait*, when he vowed to forge in the smithy of his soul the uncreated conscience of his race. But many Barth critics have accepted Ambrose's statement of intent as an adequate psychological metaphor for the author's own motivation, in a book in which his intentions regarding fiction are purportedly made clear. I don't think we should be so easily taken in. While Barth explores the range of possibilities and dilemmas of writing fiction in *Lost in the Funhouse*, and exemplifies them through the fiction of the stories, the last statement of the title story is yet another funhouse artifice—like the thrice repeated "Love!" at the end of "Night-Sea Journey" or "the absurd, unending possibility of love" at the conclusion of "Menelaiad"—rather than a guiding principle through Barth's works. It is merely an imitation of the satisfactory conclusion so ardently sought in such openly self-searching compositional fictions as "Autobiography," "Echo," and "Title."

The division of the stories into two complementary or mirror segments was pointed out early by Gerald Gillespie, who saw the first seven stories as forming a "preponderantly contemporary, biographical sequence" and the second seven as being a "preponderantly historical and mythical sequence,"[6] with "Echo" providing the same introductory function as "Frame-Tale." The biographical aspect of the first half of the book has certainly not vanished in the latter half, but the compositional struggle obviously attributed to Ambrose in the early section was later represented by other voices. Like literature in general, *Lost in the Funhouse* begins its own endless repetitive cycle regarding textual composition, and the search for new ways to say old things augments the dilemma of the writer's inextricable involvement with his own personal history. That these two problems are interchangeable is what "Echo" is all about. The names of Narcissus and Echo mean what they say, as their emblematic roles become apparent in relation to self-reflexive fiction: Narcissus concerned with authorial self-portraits in other guises, and Echo with the retelling of others' old stories with artful embellishment. This Barthean revamping of the traditional dilemmas is certainly clever enough, as is the heavily chiasmic style, with splits in sentences causing mirror images in structure as well as verbiage. Thus, the clipped aphoristic tautologies permeating the prose create a bilateral sense that seconds the mirrored images of the problems the two alteregos of the writer encounter.

The problematic wrinkle in the story is Tiresias. We never exactly know what his problems are, whether he is as attracted to Narcissus-like temptations as everyone else, whether his wisdom can be equated with some indistinguishable higher truth that opaquely forms a desired end of literary endeavor, whether his knowledge and experience are really a hindrance or a benefit, and, indeed, whether his story is distinguishable from either Narcissus's or Echo's. Whether Tiresias is some sort of aging, experienced writer who knows the answers but is unable to make good or at least practical use of them, or whether his presence is meant to provide that indispensable ambiguity or doubt, has not, at least in my mind, been successfully addressed in Barth criticism. The problem itself intrigues. Clearly, while both have been exceptional storytellers, Narcissus falls on hard, self-absorbed times, and Echo's endless life of repetition seems equally unattractive, no matter how clever her embellishments. Might not, then, the entire tale be a sort of metaphoric account of that old artist, Tiresias, the only one who sees, understands, and knows all, including its hopelessness?

The next four "stories" are presented in alternating patterns: "Two Meditations" pretends to complete omniscience, as opposed to the confessional self-reflexivity of "Title," while "Glossolalia" embodies the dark prophecies of six seers predicting disaster, and "Life-Story" returns to the self-confession of compositional difficulties by the authorial protagonist. "Two Meditations" and "Glossolalia" share several common stylistic traits in that both are heavily mannered compositions, and both seek to (re)present ancient themes in new and clever ways, as if they were retold by the ingenious Echo. The two meditations are parallel aphorisms, which, except for the conceits of their variant imagery, are clichés hackneyed almost beyond salvation: "the straw that broke the camel's back" and "the Monday morning quarterback." Yet they appear striking and original, worthy of thought and speculation, because of their virtuosity of contextual style. By linking the two descriptions of Armageddon with bodies of water near Buffalo (Niagara Falls and Lake Erie), the first with violent destruction due to mysterious, almost supernatural forces, the second just as inexorable a deterioration due to quiet, voluntary, but lethal pollution, Barth creates a sort of rudimentary unrhymed sonnet in which the second, shorter, part serves as conservationist counterpoint to the first. Instead of varying the rhyme scheme between octet and sextet, Barth employs an almost regular metric cadence of iambs and anapests to "Niagara Falls" and increased alliteration in "Lake Erie." The perennial truths are further rejuvenated by Barth's metaphors, which are varied enough to be described by one critic as "bizarre correspondences," but which might more charitably be regarded as poetic conceits: falling plaster, falling bookshelves, the crumbling lip of Niagara Falls, snowflakes and avalanches, stars exploding, tea taxes and revolution, and the indignity of spouses in the first section; and Oedipus' parricide and incest, Venice slipping into the sea, South American revolution, and the pollution of Lake Erie in the second. The ancient quality of the causes intersects with the immediacy of the present: the plight of Lake Erie, the crumbling lip of the Falls, and so on. While the story is apparently Echo-authored, Tiresian elements abound, especially in the extended blindness references in *Oedipus* which conclude the second piece. Both contain the wearied wisdom of despair that characterizes all Tiresias's predictions, made by an existential seer continually hounded for the truth of impending doom and futility.

The verbal counterpart to "Two Meditations," "Glossolalia" again links a series of six first-person, nonauthorial narrative messages to a general cliché, "Shit happens," which could easily be Tiresias's theme song. The Echo-oriented verbal ingeniousness here is that all six lamentations have exactly the same metric pattern as the "Lord's Prayer," and really should be sung to the well-known tune to appreciate the blasphemous irony fully.[7] Far from the familiar message of hope, the speakers or storytellers invite investigations of both the form of the message and the complexity of the deceit, which may be as "dismaying" as the unhappy message it brings. Barth's endnote informs us that "*anything* examined closely enough" is bound to have the same grim result (*F* 203). It begins to look as if Barth's existential despair is more and more associated with the mysterious truth Tiresias shares with him.

The last speaker, the author himself, spells it all out as he links the two intervening attempts at unselfconscious fiction to the reflexive struggles of the author in "Title" and "Life-Story." Tiresias is really the muse: "Ill fortune, constraint and terror, generate guileful art; despair inspires" (*F* 115).

Again, as is the case in *Dubliners*, each successive story carries some seed of a previous one. The reference in "Two Meditations" to the apparently resigned spouse who harbors murder in her insides leads in "Title" to the double entendre of the writer's inability to satisfy the intertwined demands of his own creative muse and his domestic life, or to find the right words to produce an adequate aesthetic response to their relationship. The story is again about writing a story, the first-person narrator writing about a third-person narrator who is doing the same thing. The woman is either a character in the frame or in the frame author's story or both. At any rate, she becomes identified with the author's own alter ego, constantly questioning, as the whole is presented as a dialogue between the author and himself, in an attempt to project his own domestic dilemma and that of his culture and literature on the story he writes. His sense of despair is therefore compounded by its redundancy; his story, his life, and his artistic tradition are all unsatisfying, meaningless, and so on, the *end* never quite written, the closure nonexistent.

"Life-Story" is another attempt of the writer to present a more traditional form of narrative, while at the same time having as its plot the problems of writing such a narrative. Barth repeatedly informs us of the precise time and date as the narrative progresses. The female is identified as the writer's wife, and the date as his birthday. The problem crystallizes into the classic narcissistic dilemma: If the writer is writing about a writer writing about a writer, and so on, does not the infinite reflexivity work in the opposite direction? Is not the writer, even as he writes, little more than a character in his own life's fiction? The problem of seeing our lives as a piece of fiction is one Ambrose has had to deal with from the outset of his biographical pieces, and if he is now the mature Barthean author of the second half of the book, what makes the present story appear more satisfactory than its counterpart, "Title"? Only the reader's appreciation of more traditional verbiage. Even if it is a parody of clichéd style, we can recognize the humor, and be appeased at the domestic tranquility of the surrender to sexual normalcy. "Life-Story" appears as a bridge among the previous three pieces and the brilliant artifices of the last two stories in the collection.

Both chronology and authorial voice remain as constant during the last half of the book as they did in the first (Ambrose) half. Barth gives us, as he has warned, plenty of indication that the author is himself a fictionalized Barth surrogate (even if they have different birthdays) who has just been writing the penultimate selection of "Glossolalia"; who has alternatively wavered between homilies cloaked in realism and the torments of self-revelation regarding the creation of literary artifacts in "Title"; and who now, although bothered that he still thinks himself a fictional character, has managed to effect some sort of truce that will enable him to be inside the last two stories, yet be outside them too. The reconciliation will provide a combination that will raise the issues the author has so desperately reiterated all along, and yet afford him the opportunity to be honestly a part of their resolution. The plan would allow Ambrose to exist independently of Barth and the two storytellers of the last two stories, and yet permit them all to participate as separate, and, at the same time, multiple consubstantial entities. They will all be Menelaus, the minstrel, Ambrose, Ambrose's creation of the writer of "Life-Story," and Barth, a variation on Narcissus, Echo, and Tiresias.

In "Menelaiad," a derivation of *The Odyssey* and the even older sources that gave us "The Wife of Bath's Tale," the self-effacing, self-pitying, self-reflexive seeker/cuckold narrator assumes the guise of Menelaus, a Narcissus figure who overwrites mythically inspired narrative as a revelation of his own history; that is, the history of his love and search for answers regarding his chosen, Helen—the Magda of the mature fiction of Ambrose grown to full narrative potential. We learn six lines into the story that the narrator is not the *voice* of Menelaus, but Menelaus himself, or all that is left of him: the tale surviving the subject and teller both. The Echo figure also assumes the role of Menelaus, bound to tell and retell the same story to any passerby, interested or not, and to recapitulate the frame narrative in six layers of stories that the seeker-after-truth, Menelaus, must recount before the answer to his ultimate question, "Why?," is revealed or perhaps falsely revealed to him. The Tiresias figure, seer/portent-reader, who knows the meaning of past and present as well as future, assumes the role of Proteus, the shape-changer from whom the meaning of how to go about learning the ultimate answer to "Why?" must be wrested.

The frame story about why Helen chose the self-proclaimed inferior, Menelaus, over all the other suitors, and why she so persistently refuses to reconsummate their marriage, involves what happened on their wedding night, replayed on their reuniting after Troy. Before the answer is wrested from Helen, the answers to leading questions in similar quests each have to be gotten in turn. The ultimate path to take in order to learn how to deal with Helen is only through the Tiresian Proteus, whose message is twofold: to the direct question of why she chose Menelaus, "Helen chose you without reason because she loves you without cause; embrace her without question and watch your weather change" (*F* 161); and to the indirect question about how to go about the search and the relating of it, Proteus shifts shapes so often, assumes other roles so convincingly, that Menelaus is never even sure, as he hangs on to Proteus's ever-metamorphosing tail, that he himself has not become Proteus, and Proteus him, that everything simple does not appear in another form. If Menelaus is potentially everything, a constant shape-changer himself having merged somehow with Proteus (even their beards intertwine), then he is also nothing, but, as the conclusion states, a nothing that can be related over and over again: his own story, exactly like the sperm created by the minstrel who becomes Ambrose, who becomes his story, who makes the *Funhouse* masterpiece we are reading. Here at last the disturbingly vague character of "Echo," Tiresias, becomes the mysterious interlocutor as Menelaus incorporates all three principals of "Echo" in his own character.

Barth/Ambrose/Menelaus's tale is typically an ancient one retold in hilarious updated slang and such mocking bawdy revelation that the whole thing centers on sex. Menelaus, as the title indicates, is the multiple protagonist, his love quest the penance, and his acceptance of everything that Helen tells him the key to a paradisiacal life of submissive solitude in her embrace. Parodying *The Odyssey*, as mentioned previously, the story also has overtones of "The Wife of Bath's Tale." The errant knight is similarly counselled into submission and fulfillment in the form of the love of a beautiful woman once he suspends belief in his own inclinations and sensibilities. That the Wife's tale is a self-serving wish fulfillment of an over-the-hill domineering matron, whose fifth marriage was, in its own embattled way, a magnificently perverse love story, affords a parallel narcissism to complement Menelaus's own. One wonders if the all-wise, shape-changing, loathly lady will ever be content to be as loyal and servile as the Wife cracks her up to be, just as we wonder at the veracity of the alternative chaste Helen yearning in Egypt to be reunited with her husband, who is supposedly chasing a falsely conjured dream. Even the alternative "cloud-Helen" is not an original creation of Barth, any more than its recitation in H.D.'s *Helen in Egypt* was an original version of the feminist prototype, a tale probably earlier than the traditional patriarchal Homer's.

The key, concluding word, "love," inexplicable but satisfying if not investigated too exhaustively, reminds us of the recent controversy over the Gabler edition of *Ulysses*, which purports to add the answer to what many critics, including Richard Ellmann, regard as the key question in Joyce's novel: "What is the word known to all men?" That Hans Gabler answered the question with the word "love" set off an international feud among Joyce scholars, whose faith in the efficacy of the word opened new horizons for them, and the skeptics, who called Gabler's editorial procedures into question. The strength of the word, now accepted as an article of faith or disbelief, rivals its biblical counterpart in proclaiming love (charity) to be the greatest of the three natural attributes: "the absurd, unending possibility of love" (*F* 176), with which "Menelaiad" ends, involves an act of faith not only on Menelaus's part, but also on the reader's. The reader, like Menelaus, has followed, clinging to the Protean shifts in narrative voice, up and down the labyrinthine dead ends of mirrorhouse discourse, hoping to be let out into the light of understandable truth at the end, the attempt expressing a love of literature and some hope of satisfying the epiphanic quest. We have joined Menelaus in pursuing an answer, an epiphany that will justify our perpetual search, even when we know, as Barth will tell us in *Chimera*, that the key is in the pursuit itself. William J. Krier expressed it beautifully: "Love between a storylistener and Menelaus, metaphorically comparable to the love which exists between 'Menelaus' and Helen, will make Menelaus real."[8]

Barth takes care to indicate that Menelaus's story is probably not the *real* one—the one we are supposed to believe—when the narrator's methods and facts are continually challenged by his fictive listener, Peisistratus, our critical surrogate in the frame tale of "Menelaiad." He, like us, listens while his master, Telemachus, it is hinted, is off swiving Helen, even as her tale of fidelity/infidelity is being unfolded by her cuckolded/credulous husband. Peisistratus speaks for the reader when he admonishes Menelaus regarding the tale-teller's "mannered rhetoric and . . . shift in narrative viewpoint" (*F* 154). The rewards are real. Like Leopold Bloom, Menelaus invites identification. Both Mensches (what's in a name?), Bloom and Menelaus have projected long lists of their wives' would-be lovers; both are steeped in self-doubt, but go through a debased, comic everyman quest for self-identity in terms of their wives' constancy. Their low comic normality invites a pity and fear that Aristotle would not have predicted from an audience supposed to identify with their betters, the very comic ignobility of both protagonists inviting an identification that traditional nobility could not. Finally, in Barth's story, our search for the truth parallels Menelaus's and brings us closer to the protagonist as companion sojourners, as we, Proteus-like, change forms and identity with Menelaus. Proteus represents the epitome of that which you can't catch hold of and keep, the slippery ambiguity which makes great fiction both a challenge and a pleasure. Like us, as Krier says, "Menelaus discovered the necessity of love for his [our] survival."[9]

In the last story, "Anonymiad," Barth returns by a commodious Vicos of recirculation to the beginning, or rather middle, of his book. The minstrel/anonymous claims, "I begin in the middle—where too I'll end, there being alas to my arrested history as yet no denouement" (*F* 169). The story, like Joyce's "The Dead," is a recapitulation of the entire collection. Mirroring the book of which it is a part, "Anonymiad" begins *in medias res*, but, as with all Möbius strips, beginning, middle, and end are the same. While Joyce's stories begin and end with the dead, *Funhouse* begins and ends with creation. The minstrel "humps," then fills amphorae with the text of "Anonymiad," the surrogate for all the *Funhouse* stories, and sends them on their way to his lost Merope to become the fictive sperm of "Night-Sea Journey." The literal sperm of the minstrel (his life experiences) line both the jug and the text that records the events, written on the skin of the nannygoat, Helen, a muse surrogate for Helen of Troy, from whom the literary history of Western civilization springs. The minstrel invokes her inspiration, just as Menelaus founded all of his tales of truth-seeking on his worship of her enigmatic favor. In a deed reminiscent of Yeats's painter whose brush consumes his dreams, Helen, the nannygoat-muse, is murdered after a long period of fruitless attempts by the minstrel to catch her prompts his near indifference to his task. The muse is finally sacrificed to provide the means of composition. In the last stages only the drive to write remains, and the story, presumably the "Anonymiad" itself, becomes as much a tale of what the story and concomitantly its parallel text, *Lost in the Funhouse*, will be as it is the *Küntslerroman* of the aspiring writer, Ambrose/minstrel.

It is the tale of composing a tale; at the same time it preserves a traditional integrity as a love story. Either the story, as the artifice of the writer, will sail away, or the minstrel, who has taught himself to swim, will become the sperm paddling his way upstream on the way to Merope's egg. In the *Funhouse* context, writer and story have become interchangeable.

The amphora bearing the minstrel's last text is called Calliope, the name not only of the muse who presides over Greek poetry, but also of the Funhouse in the title story. The book folds back in on itself like the strip, constantly recreating echoes of previous *Funhouse* stories, just as they in turn are founded on echoes of stories told from time immemorial. Parallels to such events as Ambrose's discovery of the "Water-Message" in the minstrel's discovery of a previously launched amphora that washed up on the beach provide empirical examples of the recapitulatory motif, while the continuing self-reflexivity of the minstrel's compositional difficulties, his subject matter and the problem of novel recreation, as well as the relationship of words and ideas among author, text, and reader, are all restatements of the philosophical and compositional problems inherent and explicit in the earlier stories.[10]

"Anonymiad" is the ultimate creation of Ambrose and all his surrogate storytellers throughout the book. It is a remarkably ingenious narrative depicting the difficulty of writing such a narrative, one containing recognizable "real world" events and motivations, coupled with a philosophy of despair tempered by hope and love and related in the all-important words that create, modify, obfuscate, and deny even as they affirm the hope that produces them. Ambrose and his creator have matured through a long self-referential cycle, which is about to renew itself once more in the funhouses that follow.

NOTES

1. Jan Marta, "John Barth's Portrait of the Artist as a Fiction: Modernism Through the Looking-Glass," *Canadian Review of Comparative Literature* 9, no. 2 (June 1982): 208–22.

2. James Joyce, *Dubliners* (New York: Viking Press, 1967), p. 18.

3. A number of critics have followed Robert F. Kiernan's insightful analysis of *Lost in the Funhouse* as a *Künstlerroman* ("John Barth's Artist in the Funhouse," *Studies in Short Fiction* 10 [1973]: 373). Jan Marta sees Barth's stories as a parody of *Portrait*, but concentrates on mirror doubling without getting down to many specifics regarding the affinities between the two works.

4. Charles Harris, *Passionate Virtuosity: The Fiction of John Barth* (Urbana: University of Illinois Press, 1983), p. 107.

5. David Morrell, *John Barth: An Introduction* (University Park: Pennsylvania State University Press, 1976), pp. 86, 171–72n10.

6. Gerald Gillespie, "Barth's 'Lost in the Funhouse': Short Story Text in Its Cyclical Context," *Studies in Short Fiction* 12 (1975): 224.

7. For a detailed linguistic analysis of "Glossolalia," read Clayton Koelb, "John Barth's 'Glossolalia,' " *Comparative Literature* 26, no. 3 (Summer 1974): 334–45.

8. William J. Krier, "*Lost in the Funhouse*: 'A Continuing, Strange Love Letter,' " *Boundary II* 5 (1976): 110.

9. Ibid., p. 107.

10. Victor J. Vitanza gives an especially detailed and informative analysis of the parallels between the "Anonymiad" and the other stories in *Funhouse* in "The Novelist as Topologist: John Barth's *Lost in the Funhouse*," *Texas Studies in Language and Literature* 19, no. 1 (1977): 83–97. See also Max Schulz, *The Muses of John Barth* (Baltimore: Johns Hopkins University Press, 1990), pp. 6–10, 12–18.

6

Narrators and Heroes in *Chimera*

Scheherazade, Barth's ur-storyteller, is unsurpassed in her ability to spin out an interesting yarn. However, in "Dunyazadiad" she is faced, as Barth and many of his scholarly critics are fond of observing, with a classical publish-or-perish dilemma. Added to the typical academic's dilemma, she has the problem of making what she says interesting and even perhaps meaningful. Casting about for a solution in mythology and folklore, she comes to this conclusion:

> It's in words that the magic is—Abracadabra, Open Sesame, and the rest—but the words in one story aren't magical in the next. The real magic is to understand which words work, and when, and for what; the trick is to learn the trick. . . . And those words are made from the letters of our alphabet: a couple-dozen squiggles we can draw with this pen. This is the key, Doony! And the treasure, too, if we can only get our hands on it! It's as if—as if the key to the treasure *is* the treasure! (*C* 7–8)

Those last, magic words summon forth her salvation in the form of a narrator/genie, who looks suspiciously like John Barth, come from the future ready to tell her her own stories from *The 1001 Nights*. The magic treasure phrase that unites the two storytellers across time and ocean is not concerned with the plot, words, or letters of the story itself, but with the telling of it: The way in which the tale is told is the measure of its worth. Stories, like myths, are merely reproductions of earlier versions in a seemingly endless succession through time. But the circumstances of their narration—the place, time, and culture of each retelling—influence both narrator's and listener's creative imaginations to render each successive recounting different. The traditional stories of mythology and folklore, with all their evolving human implications, demand that a modern rendering go beyond mere recapitulation or verbatim rendering of existing texts. Novelty, ingeniousness, innovation, and variation on the motifs are the substance of the storyteller's art, the treasure itself. The stories exist as an already established part of a universal, or at least Western/Middle Eastern, tradition, a literature of exhaustion, to borrow from the title of Barth's most famous essay. The secret key to the replenishment, reinvigoration, and passion of already existing fictions lies in the way they are told. Thus stories are as much about their own remaking as they are about the plots that comprise the repetitive aspects of their substance.

The novellas "Dunyazadiad," "Perseid," and "Bellerophoniad" form the three-part book *Chimera*, named after the fire-breathing, part-lion, part-serpent, part-goat monster Bellerophon is sent to vanquish. Each of the tales involves a principal narrator assisted and abetted by other narrators and narrative patterns until each story forms a set of interlocking tales within tales, each with a new narrator or narrative twist, with their multiple plots resolved by the conclusion of one of the subset stories. The three frame stories are similarly related to each other through a complex of allusion and form, and take as their overarching theme the narration of themselves.

If the method of narration is the subject matter, the narrators themselves assume an even greater significance. As Frank McConnell and Marilyn Edelstein have pointed out, "*Chimera*, though ostensibly a group of three independent tales, is really a novel 'whose "plot" is not the continuity of what happens to a sustained character, but what happens to the story-teller himself as he moves through the series.' "[1] Any critical conclusions about the character development of the successive narrators through the stories are complicated by David Morrell's documented research into the original arrangement of the tales with "Perseid" first, "Bellerophoniad" second, and "Dunyazadiad" last.[2] The present arrangement, as suggested by Barth's Doubleday editor, ends on a note of failure, with Bellerophon becoming not even his own text, but a poor imitation of Perseus's text, as opposed to an order that concludes with the triumph of narrative technique and cooperative narration in "Dunyazadiad." The final arrangement, however, does allow for certain mathematical progressions such as the shape and number of pages in increasingly longer successive stories, and a cross-referencing of themes and motifs in reverse order. The new sequence places "Dunyazadiad" in the role of foreshadowing a successful trilogy, *Chimera*, beginning with the Genie/narrator—a Barthean figure—playing only an advisory role (albeit a crucial one) in the struggles of the principal storytelling sisters and Doony's spouse. The concluding "Bellerophoniad," however, casts the narrator/protagonist as the story itself, and even that role is false, for it is an imitation of someone else's (Perseus's) story. Its connection with Barth himself is highlighted by passages and allusions from his own lectures and statements about all his previous works, as well as projecting sections, characters, and techniques of his next novel, *LETTERS*.

If the narrator of a failed story, Bellerophon, is also a failed Barth surrogate, then Barth's initial counterpart, the Genie in the first story, is an eminently successful one, saving both Scheherazade's and her sister's lives as well as providing himself with the means to end his own writer's block by creating a story about telling a story. Thus the trilogy circles back on itself, and at the same time spirals on to new adventures in *LETTERS* and whatever follows that. Together with *Lost in the Funhouse*, *Chimera* marks a period of self-reflexive stock-taking in Barth's career as an experimental novelist. The conceits in his books grow more absurdist from *The Sot-Weed Factor* through *Giles Goat-Boy*, and at the same time more self-reflexive in *Lost in the Funhouse* and *Chimera*. Post-*Chimera* reflexivity has thus far not again been so blatant, Barth preferring to return to a more subtle self-referentiality in the last books, where the writer appears again as a more traditional character in his perennial struggle to create.

While all of Barth's books are about the creation of fiction, and all have sex as a major topic, *Chimera* emphasizes and explores a greater variety of the links between sex and the creative process of developing a text. Sexual collaboration to produce a new fiction began in *Giles* when the Goat-Boy enjoys final passage inside both computer and Anastasia and she becomes not only his principal disciple, but the keeper of his faith advertised in the Revised New Syllabus. Bi-gendered team composition continued in *Funhouse*, where the narrator/writer of "Life Story" engages in critical commentary with his wife regarding the success of his efforts. In *Chimera*, however, Barth places special emphasis on the creation of fiction as collaborative effort, drawing the parallel between sexual and imaginative congress.

Intersexual collaboration will become a fixture of the later Barth canon. Max Schulz notes *Chimera*'s prefiguration of the married couples' joint composition of stories in *Sabbatical* and *The Tidewater Tales*. The stories of *Chimera* are all products of similar conversational interaction, beginning with Scheherazade and the Genie's, and Dunyazade and Shah Zaman's story about making stories. The bulk of the "Perseid" is the product of dialogue between Calyxa and Perseus and Medusa and Perseus, and "Bellerophoniad" consists in large measure of talk between Bellerophon and Philonoe and Bellerophon and Melanippe.[3] In the later novels, as in *Lost in the Funhouse*, the oral voice is paramount. Marital and multigendered coauthorship is the donnée of *Sabbatical* and *The Tidewater Tales*, where couples write books and Scheherazade visits the twentieth-century Chesapeake tidewater region to save the day for a Barth-surrogate writer, just as the Genie does for her.

A number of critics commenting on Barth's development of the sexual issue in *Chimera* agree with Charles Harris that the book is a quintessential feminist statement on authorial power.[4] Barth's first metaphoric link between male potency and the power of the text appeared in *The Sot-Weed Factor*, in which the key to the treasure, or at least to the resolution of the plot, is a text. The great eggplant recipe brings Captain Smith his ultimate fame and empowers Burlingame and his descendants by overcoming the impotence of minuscule or dysfunctional penises with an artifice that renders the bearer of the text a sexual superhero.

Similarly, in *Chimera*, Perseus gradually overcomes his impotence when Calyxa leads him to regain his own history and stature. Bellerophon's problem is, as Julius Raper's commentary on herohood and psychosexual energy suggests, analogous to Perseus's: "His effort to recycle his earlier life is part of a conscious, life-long imitation of the heroic pattern,"[5] especially as he, on his fortieth birthday, finds it set forth in the story of Perseus, his model hero (*C* 137–38). When we discover that Bellerophon is, in fact, Deliades (306), we see that, as with Perseus, the need to behave in a

heroic manner is at base a grandiose compensation for underlying inferiority. In the case of Bellerophon/Deliades, inferiority comes not from Perseus-like anxiety about penis size, but from playing second fiddle to Bellerus, who their mother, Eurymede, claimed was Poseidon's son, "a demigod destined for the stars." (151)[6]

Raper's position is amply demonstrated by Anteia's argument in "Bellerophon":

She went on to deride the male-supremist character of the great body of our classical myths, with which she revealed a fairly extensive acquaintance . . . and which she held to be the fabulated record of a bloody overthrow, by male pig patriarchs in ages past, of the original and natural matriarchy of the world. "Mythology is the propaganda of the winners," she declared, adding that the grand myth supported by all those particular mythlets was the myth of heroic maleness—not importantly in the matter of brute strength, where man's unquestionable superiority to woman was as nothing beside the dumb ox's to man, but in such virtues as courage, cunning, and sexual prowess, and most especially in the aspect of divine dispensation to greatness and immortality. "You're a lie!" she fiercely concluded: "We're going to rewrite you!" (*C* 277–78)

From these polemics regarding the origin of the male-dominated Heroic Pattern comes a synthesis of psychosexual cooperation. In "Dunyazadiad" competition for empowerment in framing the text is aligned with lovemaking as compositional collaboration. The identification is made explicit by Dunyazade, describing her sister's conversations with the Genie:

Writing and reading, or telling and listening, were literally ways of making love. Whether this was in fact the case, neither he nor Sherry cared at all; yet they liked to speak *as if it were* (their favorite words), and accounted thereby for the similarity between conventional dramatic structure—its exposition, rising action, climax, and denouement—and the rhythm of sexual intercourse from foreplay through coitus to orgasm and release. Therefore also, they believed, the popularity of love (and combat, the darker side of the same rupee) as a theme for narrative, the lovers' embrace as its culmination, and post-coital lassitude as its natural ground: what better time for tales than at day's end, in bed after making love (or around the campfire after battle or adventure, or in the chimney corner after work), to express and heighten the community between the lovers, comrades, co-workers? (*C* 24–25)

The more complicated or sophisticated the artifice—of both lovemaking and the creative process—the more satisfaction derived by the lover/creators, leading the Genie to conceive of seven concentric stories-within-stories so that the climax of each would precipitate that of the next tale out, "like a string of firecrackers or ... chains of orgasms" (*C*24).

Furthermore, the relationship between teller and listener is proclaimed to be essentially sexual:

The teller's role, he [the Genie] felt, regardless of his actual gender, was essentially masculine, the listener's or reader's feminine, and the tale was the medium of their intercourse. ... Narrative, in short ... was a love-relation, not a rape: its success depended upon the reader's consent and cooperation, which she could withhold or at any moment withdraw; also upon her own combination of experience and talent for the enterprise, and the author's ability to arouse, sustain, and satisfy her interest—an ability on which his figurative life hung as surely as Scheherazade's literal. (*C* 25–26)

The Genie assumes the masculine role while Scheherazade and Dunyazade listen, but the readers are in the feminine role of listening to Dunyazade tell us the story, just as Shah Zaman is listening. Scheherazade is primal storyteller to the Genie as well as his audience, while the masculine roles of both the Shah brothers are reversed by their position as listeners and their imminent dooms. Zaman reverses sexual roles twice in his plight as potential emasculated victim of Dunyazade's knife, and then as teller of a story that he hopes will alleviate his dire situation, in which she again becomes the passive female audience. All these sexual role changes corresponding to the pattern of narration and the narratives within narratives tend to create an androgyny of sexual roles in "Dunyazadiad," an androgyny that is carried into the heavily sexually oriented history of the two remaining novellas.

Calyxa's role in provoking a reinvigorated manhood in Perseus, by her worshipful presentations of the panels of his past, is only the first of the narrative conversations between Perseus and his women in which the comments of the women—their ability to withhold or subvert approbation of the stories—ultimately decide the insights and surrogate sexual (dis)satisfaction their narrators receive. Anteia's objections are as instructive as Melanippe's harsh literary criticism of Bellerophon's manuscript and Polyeidus's preview of the future in the form of unpublished notes of Bellerophon/Deliades/Barth.

In a way *Chimera*'s women are associated with the mystic, messy past, and the men with the explicit, realistic present confronting their self-pitying/self-aggrandizing misconceptions. Dunyazade's Tragic View of Sex and Temperament (that "while perfect equality between men and women was the only defensible value in that line, she was not at all certain it was attainable" [*C* 45]) sounds as if it were borrowed from nutty Joe Morgan of *The End of the Road* and filtered with female common sense. Zeus might have had it right when he discussed the Pattern of Mythic Heroism: "It says *Mystery* and *Tragedy*: Mystery in the hero's journey to the other world, his illumination, his transcension of categories, his special dispensation: Tragedy in his return to daily reality" (*C* 297). Whether or not Bellerophon's story is "confusion and discord" makes no difference in the grand scheme, but the failure of the story is, ironically, its claim to immortality, or at least to the universality of the human condition. "Heartfelt ineptitude has its appeal . . . so does heartless skill. But what you want is passionate intensity" (*C* 24).

Barth's "Bellerophoniad" rerepresentation of the chart of Campbell's classical Heroic Pattern (*C* 261) provides assurance (if anyone needs it) that Barth's concern with this mythological explanation for the perennial life-cycle activities of heroes (the idealized people whose behavior we all are supposed to emulate) did not end with the Goat-Boy's struggle to attain Grand-Tutorhood. The Pattern's four-quadrant summary of the circle of the hero's life and activities (Departure, Initiation, Return, Reign and Death), with all its attendant steps and variations, is no more than a blueprint for any fictions subsequent writers undertake to write about those who would be bigger than life or ordinary people. If the aspiring heroes are themselves fiction writers, the Pattern becomes a blueprint for their fictions about themselves attempting to write works of permanent art.

Raglan and Campbell did not *create* the ur-structure for all heroic patterns; they merely reviewed existing mythology/stories and extrapolated a common pattern of events in the adventures. To Barth, who wrote a heroic quest myth in *Sot-Weed*, and then had to be told by a critic that it corresponded to this ageless mythic pattern, the monomyth presented a unique problem: how to use the Pattern to create new fictions, instead of allowing the Pattern to impose a structural tyranny over what he wrote.

Barth directly attacked the problem in *Giles* by writing a parody of the whole pattern. It was a strategy that enabled him to perform a nearly infinite number of variations on the Pattern, while still basically adhering to the structural sequence of events. In *Funhouse* Barth played again with more variations on the Pattern by exploiting the comic ideas of cuckoldry, the incongruities of contemporary language in antique settings, and the metaphor of writer as floundering heroic quester/sperm cell.

In *Chimera* Barth temporarily embraced the comfort of his familiarity with Scheherazade's non-Western storytelling tradition before plunging back into the Western Heroic Journey-to-Immortality Quest. *The 1001 Nights* empowered a woman as narrative controller and hence Hero, and the obvious success of her stories to preserve life for herself and immortality for her fictive progeny demanded some sort of narrative conjunction with the great patriarchal Western Hero Tradition and Barth's Hero/writer, who was at one and the same time both chronicler and subject on the road to successful Herohood. In the second story Barth chose Perseus, who was presumably successful in making it to the stars, his nightly constellation perennially reminding the reader/astronomical interpreter of the immortality of his journey. In the concluding story Bellerophon is a sort of semi-charlatan, whose doubtful origins include his confusion of identities with two of his early victims, Bellerus and Deliades. His efforts to attain Herohood are principally to follow the Pattern—in particular Perseus's version of it—and in so doing be defined as a Hero himself. His story, despite Barth's claim of its "*unfamiliarity . . . even to those acquainted with the myths of Menelaus and Helen or Perseus and Andromeda*" (*C* 199), is still around, and Barth introduces into the text of "Bellerophoniad" Robert Graves's verbatim version of the tale (*C* 200–201), which the Barth/narrator/document-author-surrogate claims is "*a collation of the texts of Antoninus Liberalis, Apollodorus, Eustathius, Hesiod, Homer, Hyginus, Ovid, Pindar, Plutarch, the Scoliast on the* Iliad, *and Tzetzes*" (*C* 199–200). What the narrator does not tell us is that the versions of Bellerophon's murders differ among storytellers, especially from Pindar on, and that Graves's version of Bellerophon's killing both Bellerus and Deliades is contradicted by other versions, leaving the door open to Barth's having Bellerophon assume their alternate identities. What matters to Bellerophon is whether or not he is, after all, a Hero, a Perseus, or merely someone who imitated a Perseus. His mere imitation established and his semidemiGodship lost, Bellerophon must settle for being the story itself, "a beastly fiction, ill-proportioned, full of longueurs, lumps, lacunae, a kind of monstrous mixed metaphor" (*C* 308) that ultimately informs the three-part text which draws its name and shape from the monster of antiquity.

The implications of identifying the Hero as the text itself are profound: First, the text wanders around doing tricks and jumping traditional hurdles in a Heroic search for immortality. Second, if Bellerophon *is* the story, so is his shape-changing father, Polyeidus, who turns himself and the interview into the character Bellerophon in *Bellerophoniad* form (*C* 307). Thus, if the whole narrative is Barth's creation, and he a father to both Polyeidus and Bellerophon, so John Barth is, in a sense, the subject as well as the content of the whole book.

Barth's or a Barth surrogate's intrusion is one of the major links among many for the three stories. The smiling, bespeckled Genie from the Dorset marshes is, like his counterpart heroes, Perseus and Bellerophon, forty years old, Barth's age during the composition of *Chimera*. Barth/Genie, like the other heroes, suffers from the frustration of doubts about his own hero-writing work, and, like them, must recapitulate the first half of his life in order to get on with the second. Just such a recapitulation takes place in "Bellerophoniad" as the unknown lecturer/Barth discourses on all Barth's past books as well as on the one to come (*C* 250).

Barth as the forty-year-old Genie, besides dealing with his own past and present frustrations, interacts with both Scheherazade and her stories—which he had already read in the past—to contribute to the present account of their collaboration. This effort becomes Dunyazade's story and lifts the block on the future of his own work-in-progress, which will be, he tells us, the last of the three *Chimera* stories.

Perseus relives and retells his first forty years with the help of his devoted student-groupie, Calyxa, whose spiraling murals in highly ordered form tell the formal tale of Aeneas's exploits. Barth has acknowledged the precedent for Calyxa's murals in Aeneas's seeing his own deeds on the walls of his loving Dido's Carthage. But I would like to suggest that there might be an additional precedent in *The Aeneid* for the elaborate numbering system of the scenes and panels in Calyxa's chambers. The highly balanced twelve-book structure of *The Aeneid* is, like the "Perseid," divided into halves. The events of the last six books, involving Aeneas's activities in Italy, serially correspond to parallel activities during the first six books, which chronicle the first half of his life to the time when his future is completely revealed.

The structure of the poem thus indicates a recapitulation of the first half of Aeneas's life in the second half, but, of course, with variations that transform the events. In addition, the reconciliation of Jupiter and Juno, which guarantees the future of Rome and the conclusion of Aeneas's successful journey, is not unlike Barth's estellation of Perseus and Medusa; while the seemingly pitiless death of Turnus seals the doom of the old order, just as a merciless Polyeidus condemns his son to be a grotesque text and with it brings to an end—at least temporarily—Barth's use of the heroic journey through *Chimera*.

While recapitulation plays a role in all three stories of *Chimera*, the correspondences are no more congruences than in Virgil, and Barth's use of the triton shell or spiral as the principal structural metaphor aptly characterizes a progress of imperfect reflections. As Patricia Tobin puts it:

Barth's new metaphor of spatial form is the spiral, a metaphor whose realization prevents polarities from crystallizing out of the narrative solution by keeping them in constant motion toward an open-ended future—no opposite without its sameness, and no closure in view. Perseus, down and out in Calyxa's temple and reading his past but not his future in the spiraling mural the priestess has painted, knows the spiral as the form of his life in time.[7]

If Perseus is immortalized/ossified in the stars, it might be better to be with Barth/Bellerophon/Polyeidus back struggling in the Maryland marsh. Cynthia Davis sees the artifice as a universal need, but the result as no substitute for the drama of strife in trying to achieve it:

Thus we get the best of both extremes: the affirmation of artifice as a human need and activity and yet the recognition that it is not "the Real Thing." . . . There is a "systematic policy" to *Chimera*, and all the self-deprecation, tentative attitudes, progressive exaggerations of pattern, and narrative tensions are part of the deliberate choice of the attempt to articulate the unarticulable nature of human consciousness and existence.[8]

The frustrations of such a course of action are "reality" when Bellerophon, in the middle of a narrative digression within a digression, articulates them: "We're *in* a three-part digression already, sinking in exposition as in quickmire!" (*C* 157). The extended, carping lament that follows sounds just like that of the frustrated narrator of "Title" in *Lost in the Funhouse*, and both outbursts are to a large extent Barth's authorial intrusions transformed into the principal subject of the text. Yet, for all the problems, Barth further complicates his positioning of himself in the text by assuming a triple identity: the reasonably straightforward author/character (in his role as the

Genie), the author-in-search-of-truth, and its complementary opposite, the author-as-shape-changing-dissembler-and-charlatan. The author's desire to write a fiction of some permanent worth implies that he represents some lasting version of truth, a stance apparently contradicted by the writer's search for originality in an exhausted literary universe in which he is transformed into a purposeless game-player who sees no worth or truth in anything, but writes *as if* there were. This shape-changing trickster figure is the one hostile Barth critics have long railed against, and it is the shadow side of Barth's authorial presence, with surrogates in nearly all of his works, from the black Doctor in *The End of the Road*, through Burlingame in *Sot-Weed* and *Chimera*'s Polyeidus, to Bray in *Giles* and *LETTERS*.

In *Chimera* the shape-changing trickster, Bellerophon's father, Polyeidus, whose metamorphosis into texts already subsumes all of the Barth texts mentioned in the "Bellerophoniad" lecture, now bequeaths his entire being to his son as they all become part of the text of "Bellerophoniad" at the end. Barth's ingenious inspiration was to personify and then embody as the final text of "Bellerophoniad"—and hence the book—all the authorial impulses to aspire and fail, to dissemble fictions, and then to complicate and embellish the artifices with a whole host of tricks, not the least of which is his own presence as author. Without the author as trickster, the whole question of the truth, nature, and worth of the experience might never be asked. Genius has never been without a flip side that questions the integrity of its own existence. And few have ever posed that question so directly in fictive terms as John Barth.

Barth's own involvement in this mid-career, stock-taking text brings up the allied issue of time and the part it plays in the structure of *Chimera*. If Perseus and Bellerophon are merely fictive representations of the author's mid-life crisis, how does this affect their own Barth's adherence to the Heroic Pattern? Beginning *in medias res* and going back to the beginning, Perseus's and Bellerophon's stories conform to both traditional Heroic pattern accounts and the spiral shape discussed previously. While the entry point for Perseus and Bellerophon is closer to the *Axis Mundi* (see Figure 4.1)—halfway through—than to the World Navel where the cycle begins and ends, the circular reflections of the first half in the latter part distort time from fictive present to past history and involve the recital of past events through present narration. Various episodes taking place in the past are recited in various dialogues that also take place in the past, with all tales subsumed into a present frame recitation. Going back and forth between narrative frames in such an arrangement disrupts the linearity of progress, which is resolved only at closure. But the collection of three stories is not resolved with analogous neatness by the conclusion of "Bellerophon," which leaves us with an open-ended spiral pattern, suggesting that Barth's quest as Hero/narrator will continue at least through *LETTERS* and probably beyond.

We are forewarned of the narration slipping back and forth in time by the complicated chicken-or-egg origins of the stories Scheherazade and Dunyazade tell their husbands. The authorial role of the Genie, who merely copies what Scheherazade has previously compiled from Near Eastern mythology and folklore of antiquity, introduces the present time into the text and points, through the Genie's writing-in-progress, to the future. The story itself is about the making of the stories and the consequences of that process of composition. The presentness of the past motif is furthered by Dunyazade's narration, which is largely framed in sixties slang, with a comic grossness and an academic setting reminiscent of *Giles*. The language continues through "Perseid," tempered by convoluted antiquities, puns, alliteration, and neologisms such as converting nouns into verbs and verbals. Bellerophon introduces the academic language of literary criticism and mathematics, as progression and imitation assume increasing attention.[9] If we are to believe Scheherazade and the Genie's discussion of the pleasures of creating a convoluted text as the key to the treasure they seek as storytellers, then Barth must have taken special satisfaction in writing the other two stories.

The last two stories represent the Heroic Pattern in terms that disrupt temporal continuity, but are patterned after such diverse mathematical formulae as the "Golden Ratio," seven and later five as principal structural numbers, along with the "Freitag Triangle," resurrected from *Lost in the Funhouse* and literally reproduced with variations on page 251 of *Chimera*. The "Golden Ratio" (1.61803 . . .) is the square root of 5, a reduction of still another mathematical sequence with which Barth became enamored, the Fibonacci Logarithmic Spiral. Each number in Fibonacci's sequence is the sum of the two preceding numbers: 1, 1, 2, 3, 5, 8, 13, 21, 34, and so on. In the final arrangement of *Chimera* the lengths of Barth's three stories follow this sequence, with the length of each story approximately 1.6 times that of its immediate predecessor.[10]

All of the artificiality merely aids the storyteller or reconstructor of history in recreating a new fiction to replace the exhausted past. If that past is replenished each time it is relived in myth, it is similarly relived by people in their daily lives, not necessarily adorned with the ingenious embellishment of the artist. Barth's attempt to bring "reality" or verisimilitude to his fiction may well have led him to adopt Graves's ideas about Herohood and universal experience. Jerry Powell draws such a conclusion:

What Graves calls "a reduction to narrative shorthand of ritual mime" becomes for Barth "poetic distillations of our ordinary psychic experience," pointing always towards daily reality. The rituals of mankind, then, which form the common denominators of man's acquired knowledge (epistemology), become our myths. Yet myths are also distillations of ordinary experience, reflecting the individual's confrontations with daily reality—the confrontations that comprise his learning experience. If ontogeny did *not* recapitulate phylogeny, the Greek myths would presumably be of no interest to us. [11]

Barth thus has it both ways: He can describe universal human problems, and do it with an ingeniousness that makes his rendition unique. His own problems as writer are similar to the problems every man faces as he strives to achieve Herohood—to pass rather than flunk. Imposing the age-old pattern on the mythic heroes of antiquity, and at the same time sharing in analogous problems himself in the present, he can produce a new hybrid version, a new tale of successful variation, as did the successive raconteurs of the ancient pattern, even as he creates a new tale of imitation—a series of stories about the process of writing in which the key to the treasure lies in the search for the key.

NOTES

1. Frank D. McConnell, *Four Postwar American Novelists: Bellow, Mailer, Barth, and Pynchon* (Chicago: University of Chicago Press, 1974), pp. 118–19, as cited and expanded by Marilyn Edelstein in "The Function of Self-Consciousness in John Barth's *Chimera*," *Studies in American Fiction* 12, no. 1 (Spring 1984): 99–108.

2. David Morrell, *John Barth: An Introduction* (University Park: Pennsylvania State University Press, 1976), pp. 140–65. Morrell was so adamant about the order of the stories being "Perseid," "Bellerophoniad," and, finally, "Dunyazadiad" that he based most of his critical commentary of the book on the original order rather than the published form. See especially pp. 161–65.

3. Max F. Schulz, *The Muses of John Barth: Tradition and Metafiction from "Lost in the Funhouse" to "The Tidewater Tales"* (Baltimore: Johns Hopkins University Press, 1990), pp. 22–23.

4. Charles B. Harris, *Passionate Virtuosity: The Fiction of John Barth* (Urbana: University of Illinois Press, 1983). See especially the chapter entitled "The New Medusa: Feminism and the Uses of Myth," pp. 127–58.

5. Julius Rowan Raper, "John Barth's *Chimera*: Men and Women under the Myth," *Southern Literary Journal* 22, no. 1 (Fall 1989): 24.

6. Ibid.

7. Patricia Tobin, *John Barth and the Anxiety of Continuance* (Philadelphia: University of Pennsylvania Press, 1992), pp. 98–99.

8. Cynthia Davis, " 'The Key to the Treasure': Narrative Movements and Effects in *Chimera*," in *Critical Essays on John Barth*, ed. Joseph J. Waldmeir (Boston: G. K. Hall, 1980), pp. 225–26.

9. See Harris, *Passionate Virtuosity*, for a detailed analysis of stylistic techniques, pp. 144–45.

10. See ibid., p. 150, and especially Morrell, *John Barth*, pp. 141–42, for detailed mathematical explanations.

11. Jerry Powell, "Barth's *Chimera*: A Creative Response to the Literature of Exhaustion," in *Critical Essays on John Barth*, ed. Joseph J. Waldmeir (Boston: G. K. Hall, 1980), p. 235.

7

History, Sex, and Art in John Barth's *LETTERS*

Nearly a decade and a half has passed since the 1979 publication of John Barth's enormous recapitulatory novel, *LETTERS*, a book that joins only a handful of literary works from *The Divine Comedy* to *Finnegans Wake* in its attempt to include the totality of its author's previous works in relation to the past and present events, literary forms, and evolving philosophy that shaped those works. In the process, the new macrocosmic work becomes yet another extensive variation on his perennial theme of self-conscious creation and perhaps his most complicated contribution to the replenishment of art. While Barth fans had become used to his bold experiments, the 772-page *LETTERS*, written with the audacity and innovative methodology of both *Sot-Weed* and *Giles*, made serious demands on its audience for a philosophy that many critics found increasingly offensive and even nihilistic, requiring too much from its readers for too little, or even, as some have said, for a representation of nothing. Others, however, recognize the novel as the capstone of Barth's career, more than rivaling his previous major contributions to American literature.

For thirty-five years Barth's encyclopedic works have defied the neat categorizations which easily afford critical hypotheses. History, sex, and art are topics that Barth has used repeatedly in his previous works, but brings together in new configurations in *LETTERS*. Like "blood, sweat, and tears," "faith, hope, and charity," or "Father, Son, and Holy Ghost," the three topics are separable, but consubstantial, interdependent, and mysterious, promising a cause-and-effect progression toward some ultimate conclusion, which, of course, Barth will never wholly provide.

HISTORY

One of the myriad themes, motifs, and ideas that run their fragmented and often ambiguous courses through *LETTERS* is the central dilemma of dealing with the past. Nearly 300 years of American and continental history are intertwined with events contemporary to 1969; personal, family, social histories recumbent with recurrent traits like duplicity and manipulation reproduce revolutionary tendencies in a continuous cycle analogous to the novelist's attempt to provide a literature of genuine replenishment by finding new ways to exploit the past. In Charles Harris's words, Barth's persona in *LETTERS* sets out to depict the First and Second Revolutions, or

> simple revolution, rebellion against the existing state of affairs. Later he decides that his theme is not rebellion, but reenactment. . . . Ultimately he learns . . . that the theme of *LETTERS* is neither rebellion nor reenactment, neither repudiation nor emulation of the past, but synthesis and transcension.[1]

No matter how ingenious, complicated, or convoluted the ideas advanced by Barth and his critics may be, the relationship of contemporary life, literature, and the individual to history is of paramount importance to *LETTERS*. Barth's choice of form and structure not only complements the history of the novel, but ensures that the individuals who write the letters, and thus are the narrators, devote most of their time in the fictive present to attempting constantly to reconstruct the past. In this respect, the quests of Barth's earlier protagonists, resurrected in *LETTERS*, follow the Western tradition of Odysseus, Aeneas, and Dante in resorting first to establishing their historical context in order to understand themselves.

In the text itself, Barth provides perfectly accurate analyses of the structure of his novel as well as a tripartite explanation of the title: *LETTERS*, as in the epistolary form of the novel; letters, as in the segments of a word, scheme, or list; and letters, as in the accumulated writing of a civilization, this last sense made manifest in the book's first epistle, inviting the author to become a Doctor of Letters. The author, as the eighth correspondent in the novel, explains and redefines his intent and structure in most of his own letters, and apparently confirms his own explanation in the subtitle of the novel, which, as represented on the title page, lacks one important element: the relationship of the epistles to the calendars of the seven months over which they are presumably written.

While most critics have commented on the significance of the number 7 to this, Barth's seventh novel (the seven writers, the seven stages that appear as entities in various parts of the novel, etc.), the same critics have said less about the chronological matrix that the calendars of the months provide for the letters. Because of the shape of the individual letters in the title and the eighty-eight letters of the alphabet involved in the subtitle, "An Oldtime Epistolary Novel by Seven Fictitious Drolls & Dreamers, Each of Which Imagines Himself Actual," the correspondents are each accorded an uneven number of letters per month. Barth stands the monthly calendars on end, so that the dates of individual letters in a given week are reversed, beginning with Saturday and running back through the previous Sunday. But weeks follow in chronological order from left to right. Thus some letters anticipate events of which other characters are unaware as they write earlier letters, which because of the reverse order of the weekly frame calendar are presented to the reader at a later time. Perhaps the diagram of the title that appears complete at the end of Ambrose Mensch's last letter (p. 769) will clarify the situation (Figure 7.1). Mensch states the entire chronological framework of *LETTERS* for the reader, whose initial acquaintance with the chronology included only the individual calendars for each successive month at the beginning of each chapter.

The dates, with a few variations here and there, fix the letters to specific days of the month, without regard, in Cooke/Burlingame's case at least, to the year in which they are sent. Also, in many cases the date on the letterhead is not the date when some, or even most, of the letter is actually written, but merely the date it was started. The result is a constant leaping ahead and backtracking of the narrative in general. Barth acknowledged the technique in an interview with Charlie Reilly:

There are letters responding to other letters that the reader hasn't seen yet, and that occurs because I'm convinced there is a nice dramatic effect achieved by departing from chronological order.... If you think about it, you might see there's a kind of metaphor for the plot—a metaphor of waves crashing ashore on a tidal beach. The plot surges up to a given point, then seems to recede a little, then crashes back on the beach.[2]

Figure 7.1
Calendar Framework of *LETTERS*, Including Subtitles

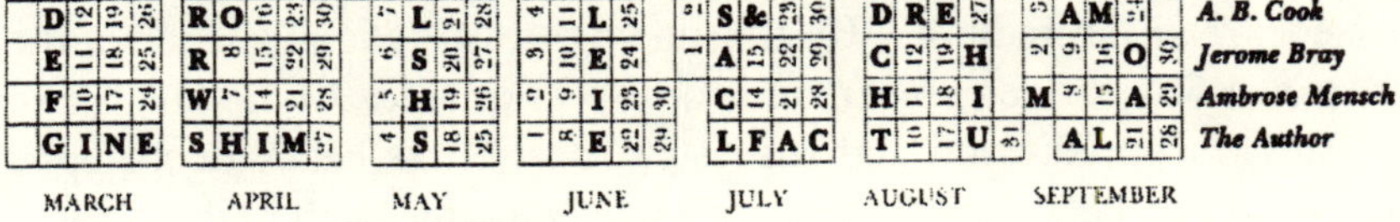

Source: John Barth, *LETTERS* (New York: G. P. Putnam's Sons), 769.

The numbers 7 and 88 correspond to the number of the letter writers on one hand, and the number of alphabetic characters in the title as well as the number of epistles included in the novel on the other. Numbers 7 and 88 are also related musically to the recycling of history, 88 being the number of notes on a piano keyboard, and the 7th, a chord anticipating a return to the tonic or principal theme.[3]

The device of anticipation is often used in music and frequently appears in the oldest literature. While anticipation establishes the dramatic irony of the reader's knowing something before it actually happens, it also involves us directly in the question of historicity and verisimilitude. Knowing the outcome of an action before we know how that outcome was produced demands a reasonable and logical series of events leading to that conclusion. Our interest is focused on how the story developed, rather than on how it ended, shifting our attention to problems of composition as opposed to plot. The account is ostensibly a history already anticipated and already commented on and judged by other sources, but the details and reasons for actions are left in suspense. We might even be doomed to conclude on a seventh, never returning to the tonic. For instance, if we would like to know how Todd Andrews came to be at Ft. McHenry to abort the bombing, we cannot expect that the answer will ever be wholly explained by the epistle writers. In the larger view, neither should we expect history to provide any answers, because at the moment events build to a conclusion that might provide some meaning, like Bray's computer they are RESET and begin a new path or another reenactment of the old. LILYVAC's glitch anticipates the dramatically curtailed action on Schott's tower at the end of the book, with at least three of the protagonists' histories suspended a minute away from death.

History in the form of the plot is shaped by six different perspectives, all in turn manipulated by the seventh correspondent, the author, about whose credibility we have our suspicions, even though his explanation of the structure of *LETTERS* is apparently confirmed by the work itself. Since the author is simply a character in the book, there is no more reason to believe him when he tells us what the book is about than there is reason to believe his counterpart Jerome Bray, who is represented as a mad author, but whom we are led to believe might just have some tortured access to a truth that supersedes realistic credibility. Casting doubt as to the reliability of anything in the novel was, we remember, a major aspect of *Giles Goat-Boy*, where Barth in both introduction and successive postscripts heaps doubt upon doubt as to the believability and authenticity of the authorial function. Reduced to the final absurd conundrum, there is no reason to believe that

LETTERS is indeed *LETTERS*, or that it is composed of epistles or anything else, but is instead all a nihilistic game.

Essentially this supposed abandonment of faith is part of what prompted a chorus of negative criticism from readers who considered themselves gulled Roderigos at the mercy of a cynical nihilist, whose protestations of the failure of literary history and of his subsequent Herculean effort to save it masked a nearly sadistic attempt to lure the unwary into hours wasted looking for nonexistent meaning.[4] In a way it is the Cooke/Burlingame version of literary history to which they address themselves, even while others see startling affirmations of life, or philosophy, or the salvation of modern literature in *LETTERS*. This version contemplates Barth himself assuming the roles of Drew Mack, Todd Andrews, Ambrose Mensch, Jerome Bray, and Jacob Horner wrestling valiantly, if occasionally quixotically, with the salvation of the novel despite overwhelming indications of despair, decline, decay, and exhaustion. Ultimately both Mensch and Barth see the actual history or events of the fiction as less important than the illumination of the problems involved: "the real treasure (and our story's resolution) may be the key itself: illumination, not solution, of the Scheme of Things" (*L* 768).

Most scholar-critics (unlike the reviewers of *LETTERS*) who have spent a great deal of time considering and writing on the novel prefer, like the most sympathetic character in the book, Lady Amherst, to suffer and live on in hope. She is counterbalanced by Todd Andrews, her rival for the reader's sympathy, whose tragic view of events leads him during the latter part of the novel to a recapitulation of his *Floating Opera* fascination with his own suicide, and to a preoccupation with the inviting rituals of sailing, a sort of Barthean *Damyata* of the controlled moment reminiscent of both Eliot's conclusion to *The Waste Land* and Nick Adams's macho maudlin activities in Hemingway's "Big Two-Hearted River." I suspect most Barth devotees share Andrews's political outlook, humaneness, and way of addressing contemporary problems. Whether Andrews's preoccupation with blowing himself away (or letting himself be blown away) is every reader's cup of tea is an entirely different question. We are too fond of Todd to want to acknowledge his Compsonesque flaws. It is part of Barth's adherence to the tradition of pity and fear aroused by realistic verisimilitude—even in this fantasy of improbability—to evoke the sort of identification that the best of the fictive tradition has engendered. Barth can have it both ways, pursuing ingeniousness to the edge of nihilism, and at the same time enlisting pity-and-fear identification from readers hardened by hundreds of readings of stereotypical traditional literature.

LETTERS attempts to explore the relationship between past and present just as audaciously as it deals with every other theme or technique: by including and trumpeting it all. In subjecting the reader to a mammoth book encapsulating 200 years of American history and six previous novels, along with a representation of contemporary culture, the whole an ingenious metaphor for the dilemma of the postmodern writer and the rationale and philosophy of contemporary fiction, Barth shows the same, nearly ludicrous lack of humility displayed by Dante and Joyce, on one hand, and Jerome Bray on the other.

It is difficult to say anything about the novel that Barth hasn't already either built in and explicitly called our attention to in the book, or explicated in his own critical writing or in a myriad of supposedly unwanted interviews. Barth, of course, followed Joyce in getting his message out to the public, via untrustworthy fictive surrogates like Stephen Dedalus or the more credible and coached twelve apostles of *Our Examination*. Critical dissemination, only a part of Barth's plan for *LETTERS*, complemented a diaspora of authorial responsibility. Barth had a dubious surrogate, Ambrose Mensch, set forth a plausible structure for *LETTERS*, in addition to the critical hints and guides Barth himself provided for scholars. If Ambrose is the logical source of the structure, each character, as Susan Strehle points out, is in a sense the author of her/his own story:

Virtually every character in Barth's antimonumental epic is an artist in one medium or another, including letters. Many of these authors define Barth's own relative universe and actualist aesthetic by contrast: pursuing absolutist ends in art, many seek to become the Author, or to align themselves with his finalizing perspective, in order to create monuments of their own.[5]

By rejuvenating old forms and providing new replenishment for the perceived problems of an outmoded art form in a world too meaningless to warrant self-destruction, Barth ingeniously presents his fiction as example of both homage to and condemnation of the old, and offers a macrocosmic approach on how to deal with the problems. The conceit is both irritating and magnificent.

Barth, like every fiction writer, is a compilation of the alter egos represented by his characters, all of whom try to reconstruct their own fictive lives as if they were real. It is a major conceit of the novel that they provide him with not only the arrangement and formal structure of the book, but the very words that form multiple perspectives of present and, with the exception of Germaine, former fictive entities who have already served Barth in previous works. The relation between their individual histories and the author's fictional accounts of them is both explicitly affirmed and denied by each. The artifact, the novel itself, lives and establishes its place in literature only through the characters' cooperation. Their partial attempts in scriptotherapy, in letters to posthumous relatives, chronicles, and so on, are but a pale semblance of their author's larger venture, itself an imitation of his Author's Scheme of Life. Caught up in such a reaction, even Barth's critics seem, like the present study, to resemble what they are criticizing.

One thing that seems certain in *LETTERS* is that time does pass, that there is a before and after. The calendars, the dates on the letters, and the familiar anniversaries that abound throughout the recital of both historical and actual (fictive) present all confirm it. Yet the events of history, even the more recent ones we have lived through, seem a part of the fiction, a series of occurrences arbitrarily assigned significance through a sort of cabalistic chronology, but denied significance by the same virtue of contrivance. Outside the book we can confirm that certain events happened: We know that Ft. McHenry didn't surrender, that Washington was burned, and that Pontiac existed, but the significance of the information is both reduced and increased by the confusion of verisimilitude and fiction. I personally know there is a Lily Dale, and Chautauqua, and Fredonia, and Annex B because I lived and worked there, but when I see the sites through Reggie Prinz's, or Bray's, or Mensch's eyes, they are subsumed into a vision that I do not trust, through a lens, like the one in Mensch's castle, which is slightly off and doesn't swing the entire orbit of its visionary circle, and I am at the mercy of the manipulator, in just the same way I felt myself to be at the mercy of the manipulators of history who wrote those American history books that omitted the shameful, eliminated the conspiracies, trivialized the important, and aggrandized the symbolic and absurd.

The view of history in *LETTERS* is an antidote, a purgative, calling a spade a plowshare, mixing metaphor with sensationalism, and making the ludicrous appear to be the events of a chronicle, which, for all the reader knows, never happened. If political manipulators now can win elections by going to a flag factory, sanctifying conception, and simply denying the obvious truth concerning crime and human decency, how much better is it to be manipulated by a work of art . . . and one that knows and admits its falsehoods?

The Cooke/Burlingame view of history as one great forged document is in itself the point of departure for both the novel and its incredulous contemporary readers. Gone are those devotees of Samuel Richardson's epistolary verisimilitude, if there ever were any, to be replaced by doubting Lacanians and skeptical feminists, ironically breathing new creative life into the correspondence. The difference was the establishment of the narrative covenant between the eighteenth-century reader and text, an unspoken agreement which indicated what incredulity the reader was supposed to suspend and what retain according to the ground rules set forth in the early pages of each novel. All are gone in *LETTERS*, to be replaced by vague rules concerning doubt and disbelief, and fantastic scenes that strain the credibility of even the most naïvely devoted. Barth had already deconstructed and held up to ridicule such devotees' belief in the relationship of cause and effect thirteen years before, when Eierkopf separated tick from tock in *Giles*.

We return in *LETTERS* to an apparently strict chronology that at the same time seeks to emulate the past, the accounts of which vary dramatically but possess enough overtones of the present to make both periods appear equally untrustworthy. Nothing is ever the same: Realistic, staged (or artistically manipulated) events all have totally unexpected, even fantastic outcomes, as difficult to believe as the histories on which they were based. For example, the massive blunders in the original battles along the Great Lakes and Chesapeake and their spontaneous contemporary cinematic reenactments all lead to anticipated but never resolved fiery conclusions, for which there are more questions than answers: Who's coming up to join Todd in the tower—Bray? Mensch? Drew? And what role does Jane play? Is she an André, a CIA agent? Does Todd die? Somehow, contrary to its literary models, the novel's concluding questions are more satisfying than the answers in Richardson's epistolary works.

Jacob Horner's writing, like that of Todd Andrews, deals with the reduction to paper of events Jake does not completely understand, and at the same time puts his perspective into a past, historical mode. While neither Horner nor Andrews knows what his writing portends, and both are seeking answers, Andrews writes primarily to his father, without, of course, any hope for an answer, in an attempt to reconstruct the past in order to understand it. It is an enterprise doomed to failure by his addressing the dead, the past. Andrews's actions are thoughtful, forceful, and helpful to other people and the social order when he saves the Bay Bridge from bombing, initiates the proper lawsuits at strategic moments, and, as an active lawyer, works toward his clients' good and in the best interests, generally, of his acquaintances. His romanticism, paralyzed for more than thirty years by a failure at love, is rededicated to suicide by another failure of the same love. Andrews is a hopeless romantic, caught up in Wertheristic folly. His quest for love is further complicated by his predication of his life's mission on a search for his own father's motives, the foil to Cooke/Burlingame's satiric generational counterpart. In love with his own demise and his view of himself as tragic victim-hero, Andrews misses a chance for reasonable happiness with Polly, copulates with his own (putative) daughter, hedonistically devises a trip recapitulating the pleasures he has enjoyed during his life (sailing into familiar ports while performing the time-honored tasks of caring for his boat), and systematically savors the details of preparation for his own suicide. His problem is that his well-made little universe of the piteous though idyllic past is constantly invaded by the present: by nubile women young and old, by the revelation of Polly's feelings, by terrorists' plans, by his legal and human obligations, by events he can't foresee but can only hope to end by his own longed-for death. Andrews exists effectively in the present and ineffectively and suicidally in the past, hoping that by finding or adducing his father's reasons for doing away with himself, Todd can recapitulate the rationale behind it.

Horner for the most part writes to himself to appeal for an adjudication of his life and guilt, although his history is relatively innocent. His faith and ability to love border on the naïve. His nearly catatonic existence during the intervening years between Rennie Morgan's death and the 1969 present of *LETTERS* is alleviated only by his journal, the record which, although Horner does not fully understand it, is his lifeline to history and a scriptotherapy for his return to relative normalcy. It is the journal that Morgan so despises, rather than Horner's violation of Morgan's marriage with its ensuing tragedy. Morgan has his own twisted and selfish agenda, which Horner's history, however distorted, may reveal. Jacob's account of his journeys off the Farm seems to possess a verisimilitude that the quasi-fantastic events of Farm life do not. His story is one of rebirth, just as Andrews's is one of death.

Mensch, the writer-author apparently closest to Barth, and the instigator of most of the ideas and rules governing the exposition of *LETTERS*, has a relation to history that is principally authorial. He sets seven stages for his relationship with Germaine, makes lists, provides the author with the details of the book's plan, and sends off water-messages which purport to fill in the blanks of his own earlier-received, soggy epistle. Water-messages have sloshed around before in *Lost in the Funhouse*, from the swimming semen, through Ambrose's discovery of the first bottled message in "Water-Message," to the floating jars of "Anonymiad." The motif continues with Mensch's preoccupation with bottle launchings during the course of *LETTERS*. In many respects water is not the most efficient means of transporting messages, but, like the Florida lottery, its potential, though not its chance for success, is nearly unlimited. The message will probably never reach anyone who might understand it, even if it survived its journey intact and still legible. Instead, it has more possibility of becoming an artifact than an intelligible document in itself, as Barth's magnum opus is an artifact, with its own identity, size, shape, and binding, but containing as varied a set of meanings as the mind-sets of the finder/reader/interpreters who discover the object floating in the flotsam of a booklist or some used-book counter. As history, Mensch's impressionistic water-message has less authority than Mack's freeze-dried turd, the latter as authentic and realistic a record of an actual historical event and existence as nature can provide—the past manuring the future, to paraphrase the Marshyhope motto. The specimen is the realistic satiric counterpart of the Barth-surrogate, Mensch's revolutionary literary message, which reaches into the past for its future exactly as do the chronicles of Andrews and Horner.

Barth finds another historic counterpart to his water-message message in a reference on the last page of *LETTERS* to an actual occurrence on the Chesapeake Bay as it was reported in the press:

Sloop *Brillig*, found abandoned in Chesapeake Bay off mouth of Patuxent River, all sails set, C.I.A. documents in attache case aboard. Body of owner, former C.I.A. agent, recovered from Bay one week later, 40 pounds of scuba-diving weights attached, bullet hole in head. (*L* 772)

I remember reading about the incident in a Delaware paper, and at the time wondering about the indefinable relationship between fact and fiction, just as I now speculate on their connection with that water-message-turd of history floating down the Chesapeake.

In discussing the relation of *LETTERS* to postmodern fiction, Gerald Graff comments on the perplexing mixture of fiction and history. If we regard "fact" as something to which we can bear personal witness, and fiction as contrivance or manipulation of "fact" or history to artistic ends, then, Graff alleges, when history ceases to make sense, we perceive it through a corrective lens of myth, or patterned activity. Graff's summary of such an artistic revision of history is pertinent: "What one does with it, in brief, is to undo its intractable historicity by 'manipulating a continuous parallel between contemporaneity and antiquity,' that is, by subsuming temporality under the timeless recurrence of myth."[6] Merging myth and history by paralleling contemporary events with their historical counterparts is characteristic of both *The Waste Land* and *LETTERS*.

The whole literary enterprise may be viewed as one grand attempt to manipulate history in search of a philosophical truth that the facts do not provide. Harrison Mack lives his life increasingly in the past as if that were the sole reality. This leads him to the ultimate belief that he is George III gone mad, thinking himself in the twentieth century. Todd Andrews's "Tragic View of History" complements Jacob Horner's "Anniversary View of History," the former seeking patterns and meanings, the latter recording chronologies of anniversary dates with no immediate apparent conclusion as to their significance, but with possibly syncretic but unknown relations to present activities. Bray's and Cooke/Burlingame's equally erratic activities are similarly based upon their perverted preoccupations with history and its influences on their lives and the society around them. Germaine provides another unique view of history. As Susan Strehle tells us:

> As a realist, Germaine posits an omniscient Author behind the evidently random plot, directing historical events toward preordained and absolute ends. Because she does not herself understand or take responsibility for patterns in her own experience, Germaine doubly relies on this external Author . . . to order the apparent accidents of her life. Her early history with Andre Castine, who claims to manipulate all of the supposed chances of history and who assures Germaine that she is personally "watched over" (74–75), confirms her predisposition to mystify the Author. Andre becomes for her the hidden solution to all of the seeming mysteries she encounters; she advises Ambrose that "there is no They, only a He: Andre" (359), whom she will later dub "the very god of Coincidence." (375)[7]

Together, the characters' diverse perversions of historical relationships represent the spectrum of alter-ego strife for predominance in the author and his novel. Though Mensch provides the most explicit contributions to the text and plot of *LETTERS*, the other letter writers are also aspects of the mentality that devised the book and its meaning.

The characters as well as the author are engaged in a second historical and creative cycle, which in part recapitulates Barth's accounts in his earlier fiction and in part advances the meaning of their fictive activities in both past and present works. The characters want to escape and at the same time to rectify what has been recorded of them, which they claim has been distorted by John Barth. In effect they want to author themselves, but are constrained by having to authenticate their existences in a chronology of events both past and present. The device of writing letters, which puts all events into the past, affords a means for them to control their own histories as fictive personages, free to define the history that shaped their stories as well as their own reactions to it. The justification the characters seek for their actions is most apparent in Bray's rantings about Bonapartist conspiracies and the impediments to his professedly frantic activities to produce a computerized *true* fictional account of *Giles Goat-Boy*, though his seasonal pace seems torturously slow, even for a tenured professor.

I have been developing the idea that in *LETTERS* history is largely a fictional contrivance. Here fiction is part history and part meta-fiction, the fictitious stories—purported to be facts—developed by Barth's own fictitious characters. Thus such diverse characters as Mme. de Staël, Honoré de Balzac, James Fenimore Cooper, and Edgar Allan Poe, among a host of other writers, draw inspiration from the fictive Cookes of their time, while the author himself turns contemporary events into fictive grist in a never-ending cycle. In Barth's scheme there is a certain ingenious manipulation of truth and fiction when he compares literature and art with their importance to history, an undertaking that seems often to render all historical truth no more than an artistic enterprise, producing intuitive rather than factual accuracy, and, at the same time, implying that since nothing can be ascertained with any certainty, then nothing is really worth the while. Yet if that is indeed, as skeptical critics claim, what he said, Barth spent an inordinate amount of time and effort to say that such effort is useless. The debate over Barth's nihilism merely recapitulates the arguments surrounding "The Literature of Exhaustion" and "The Literature of Replenishment." Instead, Barth may well have provided a second replenishment by reexamining the question in *LETTERS*, and, as E. P. Walkiewicz put it, "resuscitating that early-exhausted form [the epistolary novel] by providing a healthy infusion of twentieth-century sexuality."[8]

SEX

The frantic efforts of the male protagonists to fertilize most of the remaining female characters by the end of the book are merely the beginning of still another cycle and eventually three more books. That the new cycle may, far from introducing a nirvana, bring a new sterile reality is one of several ideas of T. S. Eliot's that Barth may have used. In *The Waste Land*, April is the cruelest month, and replenishment an image of prolonged misery rather than a fortuitous event. Although both Barth and Eliot made heavy use of the sexual metaphor to paint grim pictures of an uninterrupted sequence of calamitous repetitions of personal and societal tragedy, the difference is that Barth is funny and keeps open, as he says in *Lost in the Funhouse*, the possibility of earthly rather than divine love.

That is not to say that the world depicted in Barth's novel could in any way be termed wholly satisfactory or even positive. It reminds one of the ambiguities of Eliot's *Waste Land* in many ways, including the pain of cycles and successions of rebirth mentioned above. Perhaps in Barth's and Eliot's treatment of women their affinity is most apparent. Many of Barth's women, like Eliot's, are victimized, lamenting Philomels. There are few women in the contemporary scenes of *LETTERS* who are not repeatedly had, both literally and figuratively. When the question of his victimized women was indirectly put to Barth in an interview, the accusation seemed to bother him.

He passed it off in part because Germaine, at least, "*permits*" (italics mine) herself to be involved, and like most of the other women in his novel, she is gratifying her own desires. That is, of course, the standard sexist argument, though Barth piously informs us, "This has nothing to do with feminism or anything else."[9]

Germaine, Barth's one new character—a resurrection of the late eighteenth- and nineteenth-century sensitive, capable, intelligent heroine; companion and onetime lover of a succession of modern authors—is repeatedly rogered, subsequently humiliated, and mistreated by her husband and then by her lover, who puts her through a series of Pamelaesque tortures, tasks, and trials before marrying her. Since in many ways Germaine is a surrogate for the humanity advocated by the traditional novel, Mensch, himself a Barth surrogate, puts her through formalistic trials governed by numbers and letters, just as the author puts the traditional fictional heroine she represents through the same tribulations. Her survival and continuing attraction as a humane and realistic character represent Barth's hope for the history of the fictional forms he encompasses in his book. Germaine, who is a historian, refuses at a certain point to give dignity to Cooke's dubious, if purportedly real, historical documents by declining to offer them for publication as the product of her own research. Her independence and will do not, however, prevent her from participating in relationships that look— at least to some critics—abusive. Even if she is used sexually, and, like the rest of the letter writers, artistically, she refuses to be used intellectually. Still, sex is in a rapidly evolving category by itself. What today might be considered sexual abuse by one critic remains a Bakhtinian comic celebration of the bodily functions to another: the question of censure or delight in ribald pleasure remains in the eye of the reader.

Nevertheless, Mensch subjects both his wives to indignation, and Bray mistreats Marsha Blank, along with at least two other women, Bea Golden—an Anastasia figure resurrected for repeated fornication with Mensch, Prinz, and Bray—and Merope Bernstein, who, like Bea, is reduced to goatlike inhumanity to be sexually used in ways even Barth does not describe. If Marsha's salvation lies in the half-man, Horner, and Germaine's in her whacko-author, that only shows how limited is any semblance of positive choice they have. Most of Barth's women suffer through a blend of both past and present indignities, former deprivations and misdeeds becoming reincarnated in the present, just as they are in Eliot's poem. Other Eliot echoes include the demobilized Peter, whose long-suffering but promiscuous Magda reminds us of the women's barroom conversation regarding the prospective demobilization and adultery of Albert in "A Game of Chess," while Magda's wealthy Eliot counterpart, Jane Mack, sits on the burnished throne of her late husband's empire, devoid, so far as we know, of any feeling.

If Germaine Pitt is the sensitive victim whose perseverance merits her the meager triumph of hope rather than despair for the future, her counterpart, Jane Mack, heads the long list of historical shadowy, manipulating females descending side by side with the patient Penelopes through the Cooke/Burlingame chronicles. Their offspring—the hope of the present and future—Drew Mack and young Burlingame, give no indications that they will act in any way different from their predecessors, being apparently equally deluded, self-seeking, and manipulative. Yet Barth's Waste Land world lurches toward a second cycle or Second Revolution in a final frenzy of attempted reproduction by Bray and Mensch, and if Bray is to be believed, he has succeeded ominously with no less than five women, including the saintly if retarded child-virgin, Angie Mensch. When Walkiewicz links the replenishment of life, language, and fiction together with Germaine's possible pregnancy, he overlooks the likelihood that it was not Mensch but Bray who inseminated her as a part of his grand maniacal design. Both Mensch and Bray are, however, Barth alter egos, and, as Max Schulz tells us, "spermatazoan, not digitalization, is Barth's key to life, and fiction."[10]

In the grim world of the present, even the tragic humanitarian, Todd Andrews, indulges in coition with a girl he believes may be his own daughter. Brian Stonehill relates the possibly incestuous relationship to the recapitulatory search for identity discussed earlier, as well as to Barth's own reengagement with his fictive creations.[11] Todd's first copulation with Jeannine is tender, but the last is brutal, as Barth investigates the nature of Andrews's offense in naturalistic detail. Thus, what began as an exercise in human comfort becomes a repetition of Eliot's scene between the typist and the young man carbuncular. The contemporary Rhine Maidens continue their wail from the lakes and rivers of the Niagara Frontier to the Chesapeake, for Barth, like Eliot, centers his historical-contemporary wasteland myth around and on the water.

Eliot's autumnal descriptions of the Thames in "The Fire Sermon" parallel Andrews's last trip around the Chesapeake, and his anticipated "Death by Water" is enacted by several Phlebas figures: the Farm Doctor, and perhaps A. B. Cook IV and the unnamed sailor in the sloop *Brillig*. Andrews, who, like Phlebas, turns the wheel and looks to windward, anticipates with Eliot a glimpse of the Second Revolution (of the soul) in the Thunder's message: Andrews has dared not once but twice the moment's surrender; he has been compassionate (especially to his clients' children); and he has certainly experienced the feel of the sloop gaily responding to the hand expert with sail and oar. For Andrews, however, it has all been a prelude to dusty death, the only solution to his tragic brand of evolving personal history, which cruelly mixes "Memory and desire, stirring / Dull roots with spring rain." His choice of opting out of the grim unrealities of an ungoverned world dramatically contrasts with the frenzied attempts at reproduction by Bray and Mensch. Eliot's prognostication for the future is every bit as ambiguous as Barth's, allowing Episcopalians and other optimists a window of opportunity, on the one hand,[12] and suicidal existentialists a rationalization, on the other.

ART

If we are to believe anything the correspondents say, Mensch's account of Barth's creative modus operandi probably warrants the most credibility, since we can test Mensch's hypotheses against the written work and Barth's own published statements. Since we are given no reason to doubt most of Germaine's straightforward accounts of her activities and feelings, her report of Ambrose's opinions of Barth's purposes in writing also has a certain credibility:

A. assures me that you do not yourself take with much seriousness those Death-of-the-Novel or End-of-Letters chaps, but that you *do* take seriously the climate that takes such questions seriously; you exploit that apocalyptic climate, he maintains, to reinspect the origins of narrative fiction in the oral tradition. Taking that cue, Ambrose himself has undertaken a review of the origins of *printed* fiction, especially the early conventions of the novel. (*L* 438)

This evidence, along with Mensch's and Barth's views coalescing at the end of *LETTERS*, confirms what we have already really known: that the belles lettres aspects of the title play a major role in what the book is all about.

Certainly *LETTERS* proves that the epistolary novel form has at least one more spasm of life, and that it must, along with other narrative forms, wage a constant war with other media, notably film. The strife between Prinz and the Barth surrogate, Mensch, is acknowledged repeatedly as in part a rivalry between media, perhaps governing Prinz's intention in his otherwise impressionistic and even hallucinogenic film-in-progress. Bea seems to represent some sort of coital muse who fuels their rivalry, only to be abandoned by both when her symbolism as sexual-artistic-potency indicator wears off. Prinz's reported challenge, that literary art is dead, spurs not only Ambrose's continued interest in the literary aspect of the film (the script—such as it is), but his repeated efforts to produce artifacts of literary experience for the succession of bottle messages he launches on various waterways. Prinz's efforts to create art through film are gradually taken over by technical personnel, until the film no longer seems his creation, or under his directorship. Finally the entire artistic endeavor appears to be usurped by Cooke to further his own dubious ends, another of the Cooke/Burlingame perennial attempts to restage history, to suit the ever-shifting purposes with which Cooke only momentarily agrees.

The art of *LETTERS* emerges in openly discussed reflexivity, in which the author debates and pronounces on his intent, while the characters, as both author-surrogates and creators of their own histories, freely discuss Barth's fictional use of their stories in the previous novels in which they have appeared as well as their representations in the present work. And as author-surrogate rivals, Bray and Cooke try to establish their own perversions of the history not only of their lives, but of those of their ancestors and their progeny. All of those energetic, and, it must be acknowledged, creative and ingenious characters are in fact internal commentators on the enterprise of writing fiction. The use of epistles as the basic framework of the book merely channels their energy into the creation of their own histories and world views.

At the same time, they are ultimately manipulated by the author, who is detached from the action except for repeated self-conscious attempts to relate his creation to the characters and to explain his intentions in his past as well as present creations. If Mensch's Author is related to God, the creator in both cases is self-apologetic, self-revealing, almost to the point of obsequiousness. Barth has, in effect, depicted his work as the vehicle of a Moses leading the literary world out of the bondage of unoriginal and no longer productive tradition, but at the same time he is a self-confessed sinner whose ingenious techniques may have robbed the very treasure he was trying to produce of its own humanity, warmth, feeling, goodness, and so on. All of Barth's works are in essence philosophical discourses regarding the creation of literature, epistemology, and the relationship between art—particularly literary art—and truth, but the earlier works were merely segmental prologues to *LETTERS*, in which the whole of Barth's fictive creation joins the argument.

Nobody is more aware than Barth that the danger lies in a fictive creation that exists solely as a creative example of philosophical-literary debate. If literature has traditionally had as its end the exposure and delineation of certain truths about human nature, and if a modern author does not necessarily believe in either the method or the truth in demonstrations of some higher spiritual morality or good, then he may well devote his energies to exposing the façade of the artistic artifice that pretends to those truths, while at the same time attempting to pay homage to the artifice itself through emulation and contemporary improvement. Like all modern literary critics, Barth must first pay attention to literature as an art form, dissecting it like a scientist before reconstructing it again like a builder. His edifice is a combination of artistic creation, both Mensch's castle—resting on shifting sands, without enough mortar in its foundation to guarantee its permanence—and Schott's Tower of Academic Truth, which has equally untrustworthy foundations and an army of dissidents ready to bring it down even before it crumbles on its own inadequate underpinnings.

The dubious author then seeks to discredit as well as advance all his previous attempts at building an ultimate tower of truth, while at the same time mortaring in still another cornerstone of artistic achievement, itself destined to be flawed even as it is laid. The reflexive aspect of Barth's commenting on his own work is partially defensive, answering various criticisms before the critics even make them. As Marjorie Roemer points out, the technique is complemented by Barth's turning the serious and passionate, and hence potentially sentimental—and thus embarrassing—into farce, parody, and comedic self-referentiality: "What emerges, finally, is a created world hedged by intelligence, erudition, and sophistication. It is a space where language may indeed speak of itself fatally, disempowering its own projections as it proceeds."[13]

Barth also combats the criticism that his works are merely "heartless virtuosity"—even while his surrogate, Mensch, admits that possibility in *LETTERS* (768)—by returning to realistic fiction, inviting human sympathy and identification with many of his characters. In his rediscovery of the epistolary form, Barth gains license to reintroduce all the fictive techniques that followed in the 200-year history of the English novel. In writing his contemporary fiction, Barth has adapted a variety of early techniques to fit postmodern reality, and, at the same time, to delineate its problems, even though he knows all solutions are suspect. Barth attempts "illumination," honest in all its convoluted trickery, and not "solution," corrupt in all its preconceived moralistic simplicity. The concept is as bold as any Cooke or Burlingame ever devised, magnificent in its ingeniousness, arresting in its characterization, absorbing in its arguments, and as risky an undertaking as any author since Joyce has attempted.

NOTES

1. Charles B. Harris, *Passionate Virtuosity: The Fiction of John Barth* (Urbana: University of Illinois Press, 1983), p. 161.
2. Charlie Reilly, "An Interview with John Barth," *Contemporary Literature* 22, no. 1 (1981): 12.

3. E. P. Walkiewicz, *John Barth* (Boston: Twayne, 1986), pp. 5–6, makes a good deal of what other scholars have only touched upon, Barth's early acquaintance with music and harmonics. Walkiewicz outlines a musical framework for Barth's fiction, including *LETTERS*, as a series of fugal motifs repeated with variations. Several critics followed, drawing a fugal parallel to the diverse plots involving the various letter writers. I would caution that, if Barth were consciously working along fugal lines, a technique that had already been mined by Joyce, Huxley, and others, there was scarce self-conscious authorial admission of it in *LETTERS*, and so little that paralleled or burlesqued the technique, compared with other devices with which Barth toyed. Bray's parody of the "Star-Spangled Banner" (755) is a direct echo of Joyce's Cyclops parody of the Apostles' Creed, but nowhere can I find variations on previous authors' use of fugal motifs, except in such broad terms as to be no longer identifiable.

4. In the words of Marjorie Godlin Roemer, "We begin to feel self-consciously anxious that we ourselves are his joke, our bewildered submersion in a network of self-canceling fictive codes his real subject" ("The Paradigmatic Mind: John Barth's *LETTERS*," *Twentieth Century Literature* 33, no. 1 [Spring 1987]: 38).

5. Susan Strehle, *Fiction in the Quantum Universe* (Chapel Hill: University of North Carolina Press, 1992), p. 135.

6. Gerald Graff, "Under Our Belt and Off Our Back: Barth's *LETTERS* and Postmodern Fiction," *TriQuarterly* 52 (Fall 1981): 159. The Eliot quotation is taken from *"Ulysses*, Order, and Myth," in *Selected Prose of T. S. Eliot*, ed. Frank Kermode (New York: Harcourt Brace Jovanovich, 1975), p. 177.

While I agree that Graff's analysis has some validity, his conclusion (i.e., Barth's "symmetries are all pointless" [p. 162], since Barth believes that history is pointless) is not the only one that can be drawn from Graff's conjecture. Rather, I think that Barth has managed in *LETTERS* to forge a new explanation of coexistence of history and fictive art in the very art he has created.

7. Strehle, *Fiction in the Quantum Universe*, p. 143.

8. Walkiewicz, *John Barth*, p. 136.

9. Reilly, "Interview," p. 17.

10. Max F. Schulz, "Barth, *LETTERS*, and the Great Tradition," *Genre* 14, no. 1 (Spring 1981): 99.

11. Brian Stonehill, *The Self-Conscious Novel* (Philadelphia: University of Pennsylvania Press, 1988), pp. 161–62.

12. Max Schulz ("Barth, *LETTERS* . . . ," pp. 95–113) makes the greatest claims for *LETTERS*, seeing the volume as the ultimate "Great American Novel," the postmodernist novel extraordinaire, the Zeitgeist of the sixties, and the classic counter-genre novel since *Don Quixote*.

13. Roemer, "Paradigmatic Mind," p. 47.

8

Sabbatical: Conception Concepts in the Chesapeake Womb-World

Barth's representations of male-female collaboration in the authorial process may have begun as far back as *Lost in the Funhouse*, but they become an explicit focus in the joint efforts of Scheherazade and her anonymous twentieth-century Chesapeake Genie in *Chimera*. Both "Perseid" and "Bellerophoniad" continue the joint authorship motif from "Dunyazadiad," when the protagonist-writers share narrative reconstructions of their past, predominantly with women. In *LETTERS* Lady Amherst contributes to Ambrose's efforts in the formal process of novel writing, as well as inspiring him and in the process writing more pages of *LETTERS* than he. However, all seven putative authors contribute their epistles to the novel, with the godlike hand of the author, "J.B.," arranging their ideas both inside the text and out.

The idea of sex-as-inspiration takes hold in *LETTERS*, but the idea that the frame novel or story is the child of an inspirational female and a skilled artificer, and that its creation begins in inspired sexual congress, is merely toyed with in *Chimera*, but overtly celebrated in *Sabbatical* and *The Tidewater Tales*. The relationship of sex to writing had long been a staple Barthean idea. As he declared at Iowa, "When you begin to talk about dramatic structure, you get inextricably involved in sexual metaphors."[1]

With Barth's dedication of his last three novels to his second wife, Shelly, and the increasing attention to joint husband/wife authorship, or conception, his books take the shape of novelistic love poems, rightly titled "romances." What carnality remains in the semi-sexual inspiration of Scheherazade is by *The Tidewater Tales* merely the wishful thinking of the female masterstoryteller and her companion/author across time. Echoes of Dunyazade appear in *Sabbatical* as Susan's abused and brutally raped twin sister Mims;

the goodhearted former lesbian lover of Katherine Sagamore, May; and the raped twin ova in "SEX EDUCATION: Play." The play, about the trials of personified twin eggs caught in the cycle of reproduction, is the female counterpart to Barth's saga of a sperm swimming toward seminal immortality in *Lost in the Funhouse*. SEX EDUCATION becomes the basic reproductive metaphor that informs both *Sabbatical* and *The Tidewater Tales*. The manuscript appears in *Tidewater* in a capsule left over from *Sabbatical* and still floating in the Chesapeake. Although that concept will be more fully developed in Chapter 9, the two books are mutually dependent on each other for the reader's full understanding of each.

Barth began his career as a novelist by essentially rewriting *The Floating Opera* into *The End of the Road*, changing plot details and peopling the second book with a set of different but yet analogous characters. The similarity between his first two books was a statement about the artificiality of plot and characterization, and of the comparatively minimal contribution these traditional components make to a given work and to the art of novel writing, an enterprise that was always Barth's major theme. The several ways in which an old story can be retold inspired his famous declarations about literary metamorphosis in the "Literature of Exhaustion" and "Literature of Replenishment" essays. However, in *Sabbatical* and *The Tidewater Tales*, his variations gain another perspective not present in the evolution from the terminal nonexplosion of *The Floating Opera* to the abortionary *End of the Road*: that a good idea may gestate like a fetus, to appear fully developed and elaborated through a process of positive evolution. *Sabbatical* is a rough draft, an apprentice work of collaborating, gifted, but not fully developed amateur writers, while the *The Tidewater Tales* is crafted by a seasoned professional writer, inspired by another intelligent, creative woman. The second novel, when it emerges from the process of its own creation from the earlier book, is completely developed, with a much more complex set of guidelines and interwoven themes, as Barth continually reminds us. While each book can stand alone, the relatively uncomplicated aspects of the former provide a primer for the second in ways not nearly so apparent in the fledgling Barth's first two novels.

Both *The Tidewater Tales* and *Sabbatical* are sea-voyage stories with the sexual life of the husband/wife protagonists inextricably intertwined with the creation of a child/novel which will define their existence. But the abortion of Fenwick and Susan Turner's twin biological fetuses is not completely compatible with the survival of their twin tales: the book, *Sabbatical*, and the surviving manuscript of a play entitled SEX EDUCATION. The play is found floating in the Chesapeake by the surrogate couple, Katherine and Peter Sagamore, in *Tidewater Tales*, and eventually becomes the later book's principal textual metaphor for creating fiction, along with the gestating twins in Katherine's womb. The repetitions and similarities of plot, theme, and characterization are less important to Barth than the continuation and elaboration of the story and its making. The Turner fetal abortions in the context of writing are little more than editing, arranging, changing, recreating, discarding, and elaborating in the creation of yet another text. All editing abortions do not necessarily end happily. Appleton-Century-Crofts, the original publishers of *The Floating Opera*, forced changes on their first edition—a decision for which Barth never forgave them—alterations to the ending finally rectified when Doubleday republished the book (see Chapter 1). Appleton also refused to publish *The End of the Road* a year after their edition of the first book because the two novels were so similar.[2] Barth's next set of twin novels, *Sabbatical* and *The Tidewater Tales*, had separate publishers, with Putnam's handling *Sabbatical* and Fawcett Columbine getting the bigger, better, more complex, and fully evolved of the two books.

As Fenwick Scott Key Turner and Susan Rachel Allan Seckler, the protagonists of *Sabbatical*, sail up the Chesapeake Bay/womb/fallopian tube, they seek meaning in their lives by humping away at producing fiction from their experience, creating their story as they copulate through it both literally and metaphorically. The effort is as cooperative as the conception of a child, the surrogate novel which records their record of its own making.

As mentioned previously, the idea of the correlation between the twin creative processes of sexual union and fictive creation originated in Barth with "Night-Sea Journey," at the beginning of *Lost in the Funhouse*. This earlier version of the creative saga—the underlying motif of Barth's reflexivity—was originally told in *Funhouse* from the sperm's point of view. In *Sabbatical*, sailing into the mouth and up and down the estuaries of the Chesapeake womb/world, two progenitors, male and female, are working toward and living in their creation. Fenn, still a novice at writing fiction, is tutored on the technicalities and structure of fictive composition by his younger wife, a new Ph.D. and an experienced teacher of literature. The story of their joint journey, the novel itself, is the combined history of their love life, and its culmination and return to its origins at the epicenter of the great bay-crotch Y, Cacaway Island, where their love first connubially blossomed.

The Y logo, with a circular point in the middle and surrounded by a broken circle, adorns the title page of the book (see Figure 8.1) The image represents the locale of the union of the personified sperm and egg who have been floundering around together, trying to reach the epiphanic moment of

Figure 8.1
The Y Logo

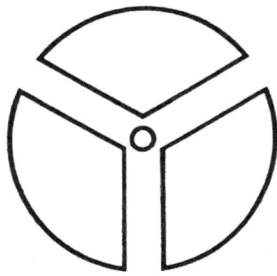

Source: John Barth, *Sabbatical* (New York: G. P. Putnam's Sons, 1982).

conception that is both their beginning and end, a variant on another metaphor from *Funhouse*, the Möbius strip circling back on itself.

Barth varies this Möbius strip near-circle concept of continuum with Fenn and Sue's discussions of shape, origins, and structure of their novel-in-gestation, concluding that it should have an increasing number of scenes in each episode: one chapter in the first part, two in the second, and three in the third, each with an appropriate anchorage or itinerary. Yet, as the book begins, appropriately for an odyssey, *in medias res*, it relates the past in dreams back as far as the big bang that started the universe and the smaller, analogous *Blam* (the first half of *Blam* and *Blooey*, Barth's names for the storms that begin and end both *Sabbatical* and *The Tidewater Tales*) that started the expedition up the Chesapeake. *Sabbatical* sails forward, apparently toward Fenn's grim prediction of a shabby future life, but instead terminates in the alternative fork of the big Y of life in a sentimentalized living-happily-ever-after conclusion. The storm as the device of a God/author to alter the status quo and open the way to manipulated satisfactory solutions has a long and honorable ascendancy from Shakespeare's *Tempest* to the contemporary novel.

While a great deal of *Sabbatical* echoes past themes from Barth's fiction, it affords an even clearer foreshadowing of the future, at least *The Tidewater Tales* and, to a lesser extent, *The Last Voyage of Somebody the Sailor*. The oft discussed dialect puns on *flashbacks/fleshbecks* combine the essentially sexual nature of the story's conception theory with origins. Susan's Jewish family origins produce a series of ethnic puns related to narrative origins. As Max Schultz puts it:

Sabbatical's system of dialect puns on flashback/fleshbeck/flesh beckons and on sailing/selling/celling, its literal/metaphoric invocations of confluences, channel forks, and the Y at Cacaway Island formed by the East and West forks of Langford Creek, and its assemblage of fleshbecks (Susan's) and fleshforverts (Fenn's) in their storytelling—concertedly cross-reference and underscore the "conceptual link between the couple's private conversation, their physical intimacy," and the story they [are] collaboratively concocting out of their private lives.[3]

The fleshy aspects explain the moments of fictive conception, and the moment of physical conception in the Caribbean, giving rise to the twins aborted by Susan in Baltimore. Two human children will come from Susan's surrogate, Katherine Shorter Sherritt, in *The Tidewater Tales*, itself a novel-twin of *Sabbatical*, originating in the Turners' play SEX EDUCATION. The drama is mentioned as a possibility in the earlier book, but it is brought to term in the later as a distilled flashback of the Turners' story's own conception. The play, begun at the Y, was destined to float down the bay in its canister like an egg in the womb, to be fertilized in the Sagamores' imaginations and to form the main story line of *The Tidewater Tales*. While Katherine and Peter Sagamore replace Susan and Fenn in the main plot line of the succeeding novel, Susan and Fenn also return as the characters Frank and Lee Talbott, whose offspring was aborted and who remain childless, but perhaps expecting in *The Tidewater Tales*.

The idea of using characters with continuing histories in successive novels is nothing new. One need think only of Stephen Dedalus in *A Portrait* evolving into the Dedalus of *Ulysses*, or the suicide, Quentin Compson, of *The Sound and the Fury*, working out his problems in *Absalom! Absalom!*, a book written and published later but about a preceding time in the Compson family history. In Barth's work, however, the continuing story must be extrapolated by the critic/reader. The names Turner and Sagamore are different, as are significant details of the two couples' lives. Barth is not merely teasing with similarities in making the second set of plot and characters correspond to those in the earlier novel. In disregarding while yet depending on our recognition of the similarities between the two books, he provides ample proof that his real aim/story is once again the gestation of the novel, the act of writing and creating the fiction itself. The characters are as expendable as aborted children when process (i.e., self-reflexivity) is the key.

Aligned with the physical conception-narrative inspiration motif is the switch in Barth from Frazer/Raglan/Campbell heroes of doubtful origin (see discussion in Chapter 4) and singular heroes burdened by problems with fathers (see discussion in Chapter 2), to a celebration of familial ties reminiscent of the Brady Bunch. Susan's and Fenn's extended families play major roles in the contemporary spy-mystery novel which provides the complications and suspense of the surface plot involving the nefarious machinations of the CIA to which Fenn, his ex-wife, and most of Susan's immediate and extended family seem to have ties. The disappearances of Fenn's brother and Susan's half-brother, coupled with the disappearance/death of a real-life CIA agent, Paisley, and the mysterious heart attack of an ambiguous grandfatherly CIA mentor, Dugald, can only be solved in an unsatisfactory manner by the clairvoyance and dreams in which Susan's and Fenn's relatives appear to Susan's psychic mother and announce their contentment in death.

Susan's and Fenn's families also provide a literary/artistic frame of background allusion, Fenn being a descendant of Francis Scott Key, whose question ("Oh say, can you see . . .?") regarding the permanence of the "Star-Spangled Banner" became, ironically, the symbol of the national anthem, a question reiterated by the skepticism of a CIA-led nation. Susan also has at least reputed links to Edgar Allan Poe, whose tale about Arthur Pym provides the couple with the conclusion of their own story. While Poe's character has his adventures interrupted by his being swallowed up in the big confluence of the waters of the sea and sucked into a gigantic black hole, the turbulent waters at the mouth of the Chesapeake and the initial storm begin the writing of the Turners' story. There is mystery in both the outcome of the Turners' as yet unwritten saga (is it *Sabbatical* or SEX EDUCATION or both?) and Pym's tale. "The Narrative of A. Gordon Pym" is reported as being retold by Poe, acting as editor of the recently deceased Pym's papers, though the enigma of how Pym escaped to write those papers is never revealed. Fenn sees the Y confluence of the branches of Langford Creek and the Turners' own literary quest blending with Pym's as analogues to the problem of how Pym wrote his own story. Fenn decides that the questions are less important than the process/answer/key/mystery that energizes the whole effort of composition: "The doing and the telling, our writing and our loving—they're twins. That's our story" (*S* 365).

The Turners decide that the events of their sabbatical voyage, on the one hand, and their own artistic account of the trip, on the other, are inseparable twin conceptions, the key to the treasure. Further, they see that the key *is* the treasure, the answer they sought for all their lives—just as it was the key for Barth in *Chimera*. What their work will become is really a fictionalized explanation of the reflexive novel, a story about the story of two writers' ultimate statement of writing about writing about living, in which the authors' lives are their creation, reason, and reward for existing and striving.

The *Sabbatical* story, which contains the key, starts on Key Island, a mysterious place not on any map—or at least on any they have. Their obscure Chesapeake landfall, we later learn (or are led to surmise), is a CIA hideout, part of an entire network of darkly ominous government installations that give the book its structure and credence as a mystery novel. The novel ends not at Wye Island, as expected, but at the Y or confluence of branches of the Langford Creek in Chesapeake Bay topography, and at the vital sexual center of the body.

Assorted other symbols support the self-reflexive nature of the book. Fenn's *boina* or hat, repeatedly lost and recovered at different junctures of his authorial life, is a sort of inspirational skullcap, the recovery of which enables the narrative as well as his life to proceed to the next stage. To be bareheaded is to suffer writer's block, to wear it is to recover the twin or doubling effect of living and writing your life at the same time, a sort of Pericles's invisibility helmet conveying the ability to enter the narrative as both participant and invisible external commentator.

The oft-recurring concept of twins not only introduces the doubling effect, so prevalent in *The Tidewater Tales*, but sets up a Bakhtinian dialogic discourse between the opposite ways of thinking of Susan and Fenn. Hers is a strong family-influenced interaction with past and present; his is characteristic of his own family's distanced formal discourse, which observes the amenities while leaving unexpressed the passionate, sloppy, or embarrassing elements in human communication. Susan and her family may be loosely characterized as providing the Greek virtues of intense personal interaction, Fenn's, the Roman virtues of abstract morality, formalization, and rationality. For Fenn's Roman patriarchal experience to encounter the matriarchy of the Seckler clan is to expose his sense of linear progress to her contingency-dominated passion. In Barth's own life, the result of similar circumstances was a dramatic change in his writing, a shift from the formerly existential and often suicidal hopelessness of his protagonists to hopeful romanticism.

These romantic tendencies manifest themselves in the metaphor of reproduction. While Susan decides to abort the Turners' embryonic child, the same does not obtain for its literary counterpart. *Sabbatical* does, after all, appear in published form. After we have read it we can pick up another story (*The Tidewater Tales*) about how its metaphoric significance, encapsulated in dramatic or play form, provides the embryo of still another, longer, more complicated novel. The two books are the literary twins completing the succession of dialogic twinning running through the two volumes.

Sabbatical's twins include both protagonists, who each have sibling complements, Mims for Susan, and Manfred for Fenn. In each set, although the twins share many values, the secondary twin goes beyond secure limits in pursuing an adventurous life style, while Fenn and Sue, being sailors, take carefully calculated risks that they are likely to be able to handle. Eliot's metaphor for *Damyata*, controlling the chaos and excesses of existence as one would a sailboat, is assiduously followed in the extraordinary preparations, precautions, and sailing expertise of the Turners, with which Barth constantly flogs his readers, much as Herman Melville did with whaling/sailing procedures. Fenn and Susan's siblings seem more impetuous. While one twin, Mims, challenges clandestine power establishments all over the world, Manfred devotes his life to furthering them as a master CIA agent. Mims's suffering the horrible, graphically described tortures of foreign prisons, multiple gang rapes, and sexual sadism is compounded by her carrying to term the simpleminded child of one of her rapists, affording her sister Susan a powerful rationale for her own decision to abort an unwanted child. Manfred, trying to free his son from the clutches of a fascist regime he helped to create as a CIA agent, pays with his own life as well as his son's. Both these active twins are the dark other sides of their storytelling siblings, whose courage lies in their dissociation from the irrational, such as Fenn's book, *Kudove*, exposing the CIA, and Susan's abortion. While Mims's and Manfred's complete stories would have made for more melodramatic action, *Sabbatical*, we must remember, is not so much a book about action as it is about writing, sailing through uncharted courses of creativity with a caution that allows taking calculated risks, an enterprise that demands expertise analogous to that of an experienced mariner.

The title of *Sabbatical* signifies more than the opportunity for a journey; it is about rebirth, starting again, reviewing and renewing the means and reasons for writing fiction. The sailing as a literal metaphor of control, of expertly handling both vessel and self through storms and fair winds, of knowing where you are and where you are going, how to do things and how to enjoy them, embraces both the voyage and the creation of the novel. Initially the Turners have run out of nearly everything. In the face of a storm and without a map, they are lost and must take refuge in the harbor of an unheard of island at the mouth of the Chesapeake, an island with mysterious unseen strangers calling derisively from the obscure underbrush. Fenn early suspects and later confirms that Key Island is a CIA base, and as such it provides the structural key to the complications and mystery of the plot. The word *Key* also denotes Fenn's ancestor Francis Scott Key, the chronicler whose account of the battle at Fort McHenry results, as was already noted, in his famous question. Like his ancestor's song, Fenn's account will only ask the questions, not pose final answers. They are questions about America under clandestine, corrupt direction; about fear, intimidation, cruelty, and reasons so byzantine as to obscure any original meaning. Adrift in such a world, facing choices about what they will do in life, and about the meaning of life in general, Fenn and Susan hit upon a progeny of art instead of begetting a biological creation. In writing their story, in making sense of their world, their means become their end. The act of living represented in their art is to be their life.

The Turners' living a fiction is complemented by their having a lot to learn about writing. Gordon Slethaug points out (sometimes erroneously)[4] that the apparent aimless sailing back and forth across the bay is due to a lack of plan or design for the voyage up the Chesapeake. He reads Fenn's losing one of the Lower Bay charts as the cause of most of their directionlessness.[5] But Fenn has lost only one chart, causing him to take the advice of a passing yacht, the *Baratarian II*, and sail into Key Island Cove to avoid an oncoming storm. Fenn replaces the chart at his earliest possible convenience, and is not long deterred from getting to familiar waters, where he resumes charge of the direction of the voyage. Fenn does know a lot about sailing, but a lot less about standard novel-writing techniques: His narrative point of view is inconsistent, moving between first-person singular and plural, as well as third-person and third omniscient voices intermittently speaking along with authorial digressions and a long series of excerpts from Baltimore and Wilmington newspapers on the John Arthur Paisley story. As Slethaug points out, in addition to shifts in narrative point of view, there are genre shifts, a series of footnotes with typewriter-symbol labels instead of numerical ones, material in footnotes that would ordinarily appear in the body of the narrative, uninformative subheadings, cross-references to other pages in the book, and the like.[6] All these seeming narrative infelicities resemble the amateurish remarks of the youthful narrator of such previous Barth tales as "Lost in the Funhouse" and describe realistically the process engaged in by novices in their initial attempt at fiction. Some of their innovations do come close to the mark. For instance, the Semitic puns (*fleshbeck*, etc.) and the triple meaning of the name of their vessel (*Pokey* equals *Poe Key* and *Poke Y*) are a part of the Turners' symbolism, since the novel is theirs. They are also responsible for their conscious decision to include the marvelous (*S* 135) or supernatural: the Chesapeake monster Chessie, the dream sequences, the omniscience of Carmen B. Seckler, and the miraculous recovery of the *boina*. These phenomena may often seem tangential to the story, but they clearly identify the text as the product of the Turners' collaboration and not the work of a professional writer, John Barth, whom we know all along to be the author. This playing with the reader's credibility, which has characterized all of Barth's work, is, of course, the hallmark of the reflexive novelist.

The entire enterprise deals not only with the relation between text and author, but with the verisimilitude of life as the writer(s) live and represent it; as Fenn says, the couple lives their story in the telling of it. For all the novel is purposely flawed, incomplete, ambiguous, and full of verbal idiosyncrasies, its very flaws are novel in both form and design, an end to writer's block and the result of a well-spent sabbatical. There is simply too much experimentation, such as the reflexive catalogue of storytelling progenitors and the Cave of Montesinos (*S* 136–37, 193), for an amateur like Fenn to explore fully: hence the longer *Tidewater Tales*, narrated by an experienced writer five years later. On the other hand, *Sabbatical* is one Barth novel most readers can understand the first time through, despite its experiments. The relative failure of the author/protagonists to produce the Great American Novel gives verisimilitude to a realistic fiction only occasionally laced by magic and contrivance. In *Sabbatical* Barth proves himself still the master of realism he was in his first two novels.

NOTES

1. As quoted in David Morrell, *John Barth: An Introduction* (University Park: Pennsylvania State University Press, 1976), pp. 146, 174n12.
2. Ibid., pp. 13–14.
3. Max F. Schulz, *The Muses of John Barth: Tradition and Metafiction from "Lost in the Funhouse" to "The Tidewater Tales"* (Baltimore: Johns Hopkins University Press, 1990), pp. 137–38. The quotation from Schulz includes a shorter one from Heide Ziegler, *John Barth* (London: Methuen, 1987), p. 81.
4. Gordon E. Slethaug, "Floating Signifiers in John Barth's *Sabbatical*," *Modern Fiction Studies* 33, no. 4 (Winter 1987): 647–55. Slethaug's representation of the Y logo (p. 647) is turned 45 degrees to the left, minimizing the sexual interpretation and causing him to see it as the "ambiguous logo" that prompts his thesis that the journey and the book are all completely ambiguous, when "no sign remains diachronically or synchronically constant" (p. 648).
5. Ibid., p. 649.
6. Ibid., pp. 650–52.

9

Chiasmus in the Womb-World: Doubling in *The Tidewater Tales*

The Tidewater Tales is a Chinese box of tales-within-tales, a verbal pregnancy, a fertility passage concerned with the creation of its own fiction. Within the framework of self-reflexivity, its analogous concerns include the imminent birth and, hopefully, survival of the male and female twin fetuses in Kate Sagamore's womb, the reproduction and replenishment of exhausted imagination, the survival of the rapidly deteriorating natural environment, and governmental responses to the shifting montage of perceived threats to all the above. The novel chronicles a couple's fortnight sail up and down the waters and anchorages of the Chesapeake on the boat *Story* in search of inspiration to end the writer's block of author Peter Sagamore, whose last name is a pun on the nature of his quest for more sagas, a statement of the threat to his reproductive manhood, and, through its German origins (*Sage mehr*/'say more'), an admission that he is continuing the ideas begun in *Sabbatical*.

The bay becomes a giant metaphoric womb, recapitulated on one level by Kate's gestation, and on another by two manuscript segments of a play, *Sex Education*, itself the saga of the love story and eventual union of a nameless sperm cell and the lovely ovum June. The play is cast upon the bay waters in two flare canisters, reminiscent of Ambrose Mensch's water messages and the amphorae set adrift by the minstrel of "Anonymiad," the concluding story of *Lost in the Funhouse*. As discussed in the Chapter 5, the last story in that collection is not only the end of the book, but its beginning, as the manuscript-laden vessel is transmogrified into a sperm, singing of love, swimming upstream in its own night-sea journey, hoping to find something it knows not of. In *Tidewater* the canisters floating down the bay pick up the earlier story's thread, this time from the ova's point of view, as two eggs, May and June, from two successive monthly ovulations, become lesbian companions. To save June, May sacrifices herself to mindlessly violent hordes of sperm, bent on rape, but eventually June mates with the shy, gentlemanly, valiant sperm to replenish whatever the intersecting narratives of the draft-play and the larger novel-in-progress require, a new, reinvigorated literature, or the affirmation of human existence.

At the same time, the novel, like *Lost in the Funhouse*, is itself circular. Back and forth, up and down, through several laps of the bay the protagonists sail to produce a novel about writing the self-same novel. The circularity is heralded by the appearance of the title page at both the beginning and the end. Once you have read the narrative about the book the author is going to write, you have only to go back and read it a second time as the now finished work. Reminiscent of *Finnegans Wake*, Barth's idea of circularity was coupled with the postmodern reflexivity of making the act of writing the book the substance of the book itself, the whole leading to the ultimate endlessly self-reflecting mirror image Robert Alter describes as the hallmark of postmodern literature.[1]

When the Sagamores eventually meet Lee and Franklin Key Talbott, the authors of the manuscripts encased in the flare canisters, the Talbotts bear a remarkable resemblance to Fenwick and Susan Turner, the main couple in *Sabbatical*, a book that also chronicles the collaborative search for narrative inspiration by a husband and wife. The Talbotts, who play major roles in assisting Peter and Katherine in *The Tidewater Tales*, are indispensable to the Sagamores because of the Talbotts' experiential example. *Tidewater* is replete with couples, including Ted and Diana Dmitrikakis (Odysseus and Nausicaa), Scheherazade and Shahryr, Scheherazade and Djean (the Barth/Genie from the twentieth century who assists Scheherazade in her tale-telling, just as she assists Barth/Peter in closure of *The Tidewater Tales*), Dee Que—Donald Quicksoat—the contemporary Quixote who forms liaisons with mother (Carla B Silver—a Scheherazade surrogate) and daughter (Marian—a Nausicaa surrogate), and various other couples and couplings which bear resemblance to the situations and inspirations of the protagonists, Peter and Katherine. All these characters will provide grist for Peter's fictive mill as he adds to and transmogrifies their stories, while appropriating them and everything he has previously written for eventual publication in his own novel *The Tidewater Tales*, which is gestating, like Katherine, during the Sagamores' extended tour of the bay.

The keys or answers to the stories lie in their analogies to or coupling with other similar tales, motifs, or characters. "The key to the treasure is the treasure," Barth relentlessly informs us. He mentions this secret from *Chimera* so many times in *Tidewater* that he shortens it to an acronym:

T*KTTT/TT*. His other acronym, *WYDIWYD* (*'What you did is what you'll do'*) is still another pronouncement about the importance of the coupling process, this time how present and future recapitulate or double the past.

Thus, in *Tidewater* Barth will return not only to the perennial tales, myths, and fiction of Western civilization (including *The 1001 Nights*, *The Odyssey*, *Don Quixote*, and *Huckleberry Finn*), but to his own previous novels and stories, just as he did in *LETTERS*. Barth simply rewrote the immediately preceding *Sabbatical* in *The Tidewater Tales*, just as he rewrote the end of his first novel, *The Floating Opera*, in the subsequent Doubleday edition and then rewrote the entire plot again in his second novel, *The End of the Road*.[2]

While *Sabbatical* is the shorter and proportionately more straightforward narrative of Barth's last paired novels, the whole of it may be drawn on to inform the structure and characterization of *The Tidewater Tales*. The point of division/unity in the fallopian-to-uterus Y, the point lying at the center of the logo of *Sabbatical* and signifying the final port in that novel's Chesapeake excursion, becomes also the juncture source of SEX EDUCATION, where sperm and egg are combined into the developing embryo which becomes *The Tidewater Tales*. The implication of the title, SEX EDUCATION, is twofold: the education of both author and reader in recognizing women as more than sex objects—as contributors to the creative process, just as they are to the anatomical birthing process.

The Chesapeake Bay/womb metaphor produces the Sagamores' twins, *Sabbatical* and *Tidewater*. The second novel also represents the chronicling of the writing of the twin novels from their spermatic/artistic impregnation through the gestation and development provided by the sperm cell/authors, John Barth/Fenwick Turner/Franklin Talbott/Peter Sagamore, who cast their creative seed upon the waters to combine with the fertilized eggs provided by their nurturing, loving, inspirational mates, Shelly Barth/Susan Turner/Lee Talbott/Susan Seckler-Sagamore. The periods of fertilization and gestation become the events of the two novels, and the struggle to write them and turn them into artistic works, a chronicle of both the difficult and perilous voyages around a Chesapeake Bay full of CIA, Mafia, and family intrigue, and the even more difficult journey across time and tide by the author's literary predecessors from the Mississippi River, Ithaca, and Persia to act as midwives. The participation of Barth's various models will be discussed at greater length later.

The major difference in the two novels lies in their respective structures. While both are voyage narratives, *Sabbatical* generally follows a traditional novel format, with a continuous narrative containing subplots and stories informing the principal plot line. It is more typical of the single unified narrative into which the nineteenth-century novel form evolved, while *The Tidewater Tales* retains the Rabelais-Cervantes mode of assorted independent stories strung together in a travel narrative, structurally descended from *The Odyssey* and the voyages of Sinbad, the whole diversity of tales tied together by a frame narrative, such as those in *The Decameron*, *The 1001 Nights*, and *The Canterbury Tales*. The plethora of stories is so pervasive that, as Max Schulz informs us, "*The Tidewater Tales* is a novel (the subtitle so asserts) that thinks of itself as a series of stories."[3] The voyage tales hold a special place in the serial story canon, however. It is no coincidence that the oldest stories in our culture, those derived from *The Odyssey* and the Norse sagas, hold a mythical place in the literature, since even death in maritime cultures is conceived of in terms of an eternal voyage, and the sea the "great mother" or source of life from earliest times to the age of Darwin's theory of evolution. Life's adventures have a mythic affinity with voyages from point to point, until the mariner sets sail on the final voyage into eternity. Barth continually develops the traffic of crossed paths or journeys of his character/narrators, as they pause to exchange stories and recognize similarities before sailing off into immortality.

Barth thus adds to the ancient traditions the reflexive complication of using diverse tales to provide the substance of Sagamore's book, in which Peter records his rewriting the characters' and his own narratives into a single plot. The grand scheme is a contemporary story about refashioning the tales of antiquity with a modern twist, in effect not unlike some of Barth's former novelistic attempts (*Sot-Weed*, *Chimera*, and *LETTERS*) to replenish traditional forms of literature with a contemporary point of view.

The reproductive process is therefore continued, with each new generation recapitulating itself and its predecessors in such a way as to add its own contemporary experience to the evolutionary record of literature and human history. The chronology works two ways in *Tidewater*. Sagamore, like *Chimera*'s Scheherazade, is working to relieve a potentially fatal writer's block, and, reversing the pattern in *Chimera* where the modern writer returns to aid his ancient counterpart, Scheherazade comes from the past along with her more recent classical tale-telling colleagues to give substance to the narrative that will become *The Tidewater Tales*.

The birthing complications are psychological, historical, familial, and societal. Faced with writer's block, formerly successful novelist Peter Sagamore sets out, with the aid of his wife, to recapture the fictive muse. His family as well as hers are somehow inextricably linked with the CIA. His familial problems involve reconciliation with his son, hers with overprotective parents. In *Tidewater* the suspense over the actual birth and survival of the children is far more compelling than it is in the earlier novel, where Susan's pregnancy is barely hinted at during most of the book, and her abortion is reported almost as a flashback. Saving the children in *Tidewater* is of paramount importance, almost overshadowing in magnitude the birthing of a new novel. The two creative, congruent acts combine in one single metaphoric theme. The irony is that, since we have *The Tidewater Tales* in hand, we know that it has been born, that the block has been broken, and that the course of the fiction is merely an extended description of its birthing process. Yet the separation of self-reflexivity from realism is such that we are always concerned about the outcome of the actual (fictive) twins, because we know how existentially grim Barth's early outlook was by the disastrous results of Rennie's pregnancy in *The End of the Road*. Pushing back the limits of confinement—not playing it safe, but venturing out into the bay for yet another week or more, and thus amassing the materials as well as inspiration for the novel—follows the singular insistence throughout Barth's career of wanting to have it all: the human response to realistic situations, the intellectual response to fictive contrivance, the determination to use the old—the exhausted—modes in an attempt to replenish them. Together they demonstrate his "passionate virtuosity," a phrase Charles B. Harris borrowed from Barth himself.[4]

Barth has always been concerned with societal problems, but usually his answers to them are parodic or even farcical. It was not until *LETTERS* that he began treating them with a less distanced attitude—perhaps because of some criticism that he was callous to worldly issues—in the process becoming more "socially concerned." The turds floating down the Chesapeake at the end of *LETTERS* foreshadow the toxic waste and pollutants that play a major role in the environmental subplot of the frame story of *The Tidewater Tales*—the way in which Peter regains his fictive voice at the same time the twins are born. The decision to bring children into an imperfect world polluted with corruption, lies, warfare, greed, and hostility, in addition to toxic waste, involves a helpless propensity to create, a heeding of the call of love which overwhelms sperm and egg despite their rational self-admonitions against such a reckless course of action: all drives and compulsions are analogues to those that rule and motivate the writer.

That the Sagamore issue will be fraternal twins, a boy and a girl, is part of the doubling metaphor of the novel, a book which, like sex, requires coupling with a mate who is both muse/facilitator and cocreator. Besides their mutual love for each other and for fiction, to sustain their creative effort Peter and Katherine are surrounded by a whole host of muses and facilitators, an extended family of good and bad relatives, characters from Barth's books and classical fiction, and friends, who bear striking resemblances to their fictive counterparts in earlier works. There is so much support, so much sweetness and light, that it almost sounds like the sentimentality of Dickens or Dostoevsky.

Barth creates twin families in *The Tidewater Tales*, one of blood relatives and one of literary-predecessor relatives. These characters pair off in parallel situations to shape the reflexive plot and character complications. They act in and out of present and past time and provide a future for both the present characters and for traditional stories, ensuring the creation of both *The Tidewater Tales* and a literature constantly sustained and replenished by the novelty of its own recreation. As Barth has built on his own previous novel, so will Peter and his colleagues in collaboration rewrite, elaborate, and extend some of the major classics of Western civilization. Don Quixote will be given a sort of *Flying Dutchman* immortality, as will Odysseus and his new girlfriend, Nausicaa, Penelope and her lover (Homer, the former minstrel), and the middle-aged Scheherazade—all, like Barth/Peter, becoming sailors on the Chesapeake. Their stories will interweave to become the omnibus cross-fertilization that evolves into *The Tidewater Tales*.

Nearly all the women of the book serve some aspect of the muse/generator role, but it is a task shared with the hero/authors from Odysseus to Huck Finn, and from Talbott to Sagamore. In Barth's early novels, the making of fiction, at least in rough draft, was largely the work of a solitary writer, but since *Chimera*, creativity and inspiration have become a public enterprise. In *Tidewater* the joint process begins with Katherine's demand that writer's-blocked Peter tell her a story, as a sort of verbal cathartic to start the natural flow of fiction once more. Rather than make fiction from his experiences with the confidential and shameful revelations of the CIA that Doug Townsend has confided in him, Peter's fictive voice had become so increasingly limited that eventually he could only squeeze out a one-note story entitled "B flat," and then only silence. In assaulting the verbal constipation, Kate and Peter begin with the rag and bone shop of simple stories—jokes and acronyms essentially—whose punch lines foreshadow coming tales, themes, and motifs throughout the novel at the same time that they lead to immediate elaborations. The logorrhea of tale on tale, all interconnected, flows faster and faster until the obstructive CIA revelations, along with everything else, pour forth in rich profusion.

The supporting roles played by family members are represented either in jaundiced or in saccharine terms. At its worst moments, the familial frame saga sounds like one of Chevy Chase's Griswald family vacations, as the Sagamores sail down the bay closely followed by Katherine's mother, father, brother, and obstetrician, along with the doctor's midwife-wife and assorted servants and friends, all bearing gifts and a constant stream of supplies including gourmet hors d'oeuvres, fine wines, and so on. While such orgies of socializing have traditionally provided the occasion of tale-telling as they do in *Tidewater*, every meal seems ritualistically oriented, with detailed lists of food and drink like epic roll calls.

Even when Peter is alone with his wife or his brother-in-law, such items of fare as hot dogs are painstakingly described. The structure of Barth's accounts of sailing and seamanship, interspersed with equally long passages of meal preparation, resembles the seamanship details sprinkled with whale mutilations in *Moby Dick*, with the search for the ultimate leviathan in Melville becoming the quest for the enormous fiction, *The Tidewater Tales* itself.

Peter chooses an apt collaborator in Kate, a storyteller and founder of ASPS (American Society for the Preservation of Storytelling). Their joint narrative voice continuously shifts among third-person, first-person singular, and first-plural. Katherine initiates the voyage and the tales, is responsible for key associations in the novel, and is the chief representative of the new feminist bent Barth has injected into his work. Lady Amherst of *LETTERS* typified the best of the literary products of yesteryear, admittedly inserted to give *LETTERS* a taste of humanity and provide a person of intelligence, energy, accomplishment, and near perfect character for the principal love interest in the novel. Kate Sagamore enhances the tradition begun by Lady Amherst as an activist allowed to initiate as well as to be acted upon. The same holds true for some of the other women. However, for all his new attempts to recognize the potential of women to fulfill roles other than those demanded by male stereotyping, Barth viscerally appeases his old-boy readers by casting the carnally enthusiastic Kate and her surrogates, Lee and Diana, all in gratifying, magnificent bodies in various stages of the reproductive process, and repeatedly cleaving them unto their respective heroes. With the best of both possible worlds, they seem collectively to provide a stereotype of the perfect mate in this novel where everything good emanates in or by couples; the goodhearted but destined-to-be-solitary lesbian, May, is a little too plump; and the wise, sensual conjure-woman/mother is a little worn in the treads for a romantic attachment. Nevertheless, the seven principal women do get together on the lashed "rafts" to jointly advance the modern tale of Scheherazade, the great female ur-yarnspinner of Barth's fiction. The women's process of discovery and disclosure, like the making of *Tidewater*, is a collaborative group venture into feminist collective thinking, like a Barthean quilting bee, as opposed to Penelope's individualistic tapestry weaving. In Barth even Penelope's solitary art becomes a joint weaving and unweaving venture with her minstrel/lover, Homer, whose parallel verses of their history as lovers are never revealed until *Tidewater* unlocks the secret.

Multiple authorship is but one effect of the doubling or chiasmatic basis of the novel. The couples' predominantly joint composition of narratives (the duet motif) is interrupted occasionally by individual solo motifs and quartets of two couples, but culminates in choral narratives such as the women's chorus when the "rafts" are lashed together into an "island." Always, even in solo narratives, there is a listener who collaborates, adds, refines, or comments. The narratives depend on counterpoint or the reflection of one theme, word, character, or narrative on another. This counterpoint may be across time, as with the introduction of ancient stories modified by the present, or present narratives modified by the past. The contrapuntal technique also exists in complementary characters, such as the husband/wife protagonists of *Sabbatical* and *The Tidewater Tales*, and in time sequences involving the immediate past/present. For instance, *Sabbatical* ends with the storm on Sunday, June 15, 1980, the same storm that on the same Sunday opens *The Tidewater Tales*. Each novel has beginning and ending chiastic storms, entitled "Blam" and "Blooey." *Sabbatical*'s "Blooey" is *Tidewater*'s "Blam." These violent storms, which apparently signal the beginning and closure of the narrative, are really part of a continuing sequence in which past and present inform each other.

As Max Schultz points out, in this ultimate gestational novel, the comic binary names accorded the twin fetuses—"Arts and Sciences," "Wash and Wear," "Renaissance and Reformation," "Hide and Seek," and so on—are constant reminders of the rampant doubling in the novel.[5] Couples are paired, relatives are paired, and even hats are paired. In *Sabbatical* Fenwick Turner loses his *boina*, or symbol of creative inspiration, just as does Frank Talbott in the later novel. The hat is found by Peter Sagamore and returned to Talbott only after Peter has used it to help clear his own writer's block.

Doubling is also linked to time in the writing process when Peter creates a manuscript, resembling a ship's log, out of notes he makes on events that occurred the previous day. The process results in a constant reference to the word *yesterday* interspersed with current events, as recent history fades in and out of the present in the narrative line, just as it does in the calendar sequence of *LETTERS*.

In still another example of historical doubling, Barth not only borrows from the great classics of Western literature, but also makes explicit references to his own previous works and implicit references to analogous situations in his earlier novels. The process includes a whole series of approximate correspondences among characters past and present. Peter's family, for instance, were similar to Ambrose Mensch's, except that Peter's people were boat builders rather than stone masons. The canisters Peter finds are reminiscent of the water-message Ambrose finds in *Lost in the Funhouse*, as well as the minstrel's message mentioned earlier. Barth finds his way back and forth among his own works with ease, fulfilling prophesies he made in earlier works by providing answers in later ones.

Besides *Sabbatical*, the other Barth work on which *Tidewater* draws most heavily is *Chimera*. *Tidewater*'s analogy of authorial cooperation between Djean and Scheherazade and between Peter and Katherine enhances the sexual nature of Scheherazade's relationship with the Genie in "Dunyazadiad." In *Tidewater* Peter has muses in both eras at the same time Barth plays with the close connection between himself and Djean in a sort of multiple catch-the-author's-own-signature reflexivity. Peter needs Katherine's assistance to break his writer's block, and he needs Scheherazade's almost *deus ex machina* presence to bring closure to his long and complicated story.

The closure of the frame tale dilemma, the safe birth of the twins, is accomplished easily, as Jack Bass (another Barth double) delivers them. Bringing all the other stories to satisfactory happy conclusions, a considerably more difficult task, is accomplished by a nearly interminable reprise of the history of all the characters who participate in the present events of the novel. In his coda, entitled "The Ending," Barth parodies the sort of well-made closure that nearly destroyed the credibility of hundreds of novels during the last part of the nineteenth century. His comic artificiality serves Barth well in casting postmodern doubt on the whole enterprise, even as its forced certitude comically appeases those things which we know must always remain ambiguous. Max Schulz best summarizes the conclusion:

As Peter and Katherine admit, "Though it's still our story, somehow Djean's the source; M.J.'s [May Jump] the voice (if you're [Scheherazade] getting this message, it's May you're hearing, at the end of June); and the indispensable medium is C.B S. [Carla B Silver] (Call back Scheherazade!), who adds items of her own to the signal" (642). Thus, in a blaze of puns, and CB intertextual multi-time-zoned hookups, *The Tidewater Tales* concludes "this wrap-up inventory" (654) of its "coupled viewpoint" (643) with Scheherazade "our projected narrator" (654), ever redivivus through the "omniscopic point of view" of the *deus artifex* of Barth's Djean.[6]

Djean is as close to Barth himself as we will ever get, a sort of Hitchcock silhouette or momentary appearance in the background—still another image or mask put on the already numerous disguises of the multiple narrative voices of *The Tidewater Tales*. However close to or far removed from its maker, the novel represents the work of a reasonably happy, domesticated, one might almost be tempted to say mellowing, sensibility.

NOTES

1. Robert Alter, *Partial Magic: The Novel as a Self-Conscious Genre* (Berkeley: University of California Press, 1975).

2. Heide Ziegler, *John Barth* (New York: Methuen, 1987), convincingly develops the thesis that all Barth's books are essentially pairs of complementary novels, each set stating, then further developing, a single controlling idea or metaphor. Also see my discussion in Chapters 1 and 8.

3. Max F. Schulz, *The Muses of John Barth* (Baltimore: Johns Hopkins University Press, 1990), pp. 151–52.

4. Charles B. Harris, *Passionate Virtuosity: The Fiction of John Barth* (Urbana: University of Illinois Press, 1983), p. 3. Harris quotes the phrase from an interview Barth granted Alan Prince ("An Interview with John Barth," *Prism* [Spring 1968]: 42–62).

5. Schulz, *The Muses of John Barth*, p. 153.

6. Ibid., p. 165.

10

Replenishment and Reproduction: *The Last Voyage of Somebody the Sailor*

Most of John Barth's works take place on or near navigable water, especially the Chesapeake Bay. Only two books, *The End of the Road* and *Giles Goat-Boy*, do not involve boats or over-seas journeys. *The Floating Opera* has as its basis an extended nautical metaphor, while Eben's *Sot-Weed Factor* journey to the New World involves numerous Sinbad-like rescues and maroonments, plank-walking, pirate rape, and similar escapades. "Night-Sea Journey" is the first of several *Lost in the Funhouse* stories concerning the sea, including modern versions of ancient Greek voyages in "Menelaiad" and "Anonymiad." Two of the three *Chimera* stories likewise involve classical voyages, and most of *LETTERS*, *Sabbatical*, and *The Tidewater Tales* take place on the Chesapeake and its tributaries. Nevertheless, Barth has fictionally sailed a long way since his first voyage aboard the old *Floating Opera*, figuratively recalled in the leaking rowboat of Behler's youthful initiation in *The Last Voyage of Somebody the Sailor*.

Thus, it is not inaccurate to say that *The Last Voyage* is Barth's seventh voyage fiction, complementing in name and action the seven voyages of Sinbad, upon whose tales the book is constructed. The novel involves assorted similarities and parallels of character and narrative between William Behler, also called Somebody, and Sinbad of *The 1001 Nights*. Their stories, serially narrated on successive evenings at the traditional banquets held in Sinbad's house and interspersed with narratives by other characters, gradually merge throughout the seven evenings into each other, until they become mutually informing segments of Scheherazade's final tale. In the principal story, Behler, magically transported from a life twenty centuries after Sinbad's time, tells of his own life's history—beginning chronologically far in advance of Sinbad's quests—and of Behler's eagerness to return to his own time. The entire narrative, including Behler's brief and then extended visits to the Arabian past, is encapsulated in the frame narrative, told by Behler to his young female doctor in a twentieth-century hospital on the Eastern Shore of Maryland. Behler's story involves Scheherazade's final days of a long and, in old age, painful life, when, courting death instead of life as she did in her original stories, she tells the story of Behler himself, transported back to old Baghdad. She hopes her story will be of sufficient interest to Death, "The Destroyer of Delights and Severer of Societies," so that he might finally take Scheherazade with him on the final journey. The history of Behler's life and emergence in ancient Baghdad, "The Last Voyage of Somebody the Sailor," is, then, the third narrative frame of the novel, involving principally a sort of storytelling competition between Sinbad and Behler, who by now has become in local parlance "Somebody the Sailor," or "Somebody the Still-stranded."

Somebody's after-dinner tales initially concern events, or voyages, taking place on his seventh, fourteenth, forty-second, and fiftieth birthdays, the last extending into his second venture into Scheherazade's era, and, with minor lapses and references to present time, continuing in Arabia until his miraculous reemergence into the modern world of the Chesapeake hospital. The fifth, sixth, and seventh Behler/Somebody voyages meld with and inform Sinbad's mutual retelling of his seven voyages, until Sinbad's last, projected (seventh) voyage is undertaken by Behler/Somebody, instead of Sinbad, whose arduous previous seagoing adventures lead him to want no more than to retire to the desert, far from the trials the ocean invariably brings.

Following the temporal example of "Dunyazadiad," in *Chimera*, Behler's traditional knowledge of Sinbad, gained through his reading of *The 1001 Nights*, is dramatically altered by what he experiences in Arabia as well as by the modern perspective and verbalization Behler brings to his own narrative. Once again Barth turns a literature of exhaustion into a literature of replenishment. In the process, he produces in *The Seventh Voyage* the most compelling realistic fiction of his career. The scenes of Behler's youth, his first sexual encounters with Daisy, and especially the breakup of his marriage and the psychological horror of the Caribbean cruise are so painfully vivid that one can't help thinking that Barth himself must have experienced them first hand. Perhaps himself blending fiction with personal history, Barth has his surrogate, Behler, write a half-fictionalized account of his own life-adventures for a more popular audience and achieve some notoriety for his accomplishment.[1]

While Barth and Behler share many of the same characteristics, Sinbad and Behler share even more. They are primarily storytellers, delighting in the retelling of their own lives. We hear directly at several points during the narrative that Behler has somewhat altered or changed the actual events and the recitation of them by others, especially Sinbad. Sinbad also colors his own tales to suit his purposes. Just how much their accounts of reality are altered remains a somewhat unresolved issue, but we come to realize that Sinbad's version of the first six stories leaves out a lot of his own disreputable behavior and ignoble motivation. While Behler seemingly freely admits his faults and lusts, we come to suspect that Sinbad's ever-darkening psyche, capable of committing incest, murder, and a host of other atrocities, is in some way related to Behler's relatively minor offenses of adultery and lust, in that their fictionalized accounts are subject to the agendas of their creators. Behler is, after all, in love and engaged in constant carnality with Yasmin, Sinbad's daughter, who bears a striking resemblance to Behler's own daughter, Julliet, about whom, he hints, he harbors occasional unsavory thoughts.

In *The Arabian Nights*, on successive evenings Sinbad the Sailor tells the story of his voyages to Sinbad the Porter, a sort of stay-at-home alter ego to the restless Sailor. In the Ithaca episode of one of Barth's favorite books, *Ulysses*, just before Bloom enters the sleep that will conclude his day, he is accompanied in his dozing travel dreams by Sinbad the Sailor, Tinbad the Tailor, and, among others, Binbad the Bailer—a Behler homonym. Bloom falls asleep thinking of those ancillary characters, the auks, and the roc's egg. There is some indication that both the *Ulysses* dream and Barth's entire narration might be one grand night-sea journey into the subconscious. During his childhood Behler does rock back and forth between two worlds and at night between two minds. As a youngster he also talks to his dead twin sister, recreating for the deceased Bijou's benefit everything that happened to him. His preoccupation with her includes the idea that they had had an intimate exchange of narratives even in the womb. The obsession leads to the confessional motif that permeates his subsequent writing, and to his present recitation of his story to a female-doctor/full-grown-sister-surrogate, for whose ears he rehearses virtually the entire tale of his life. Several of Behler's lovers are also tied into the sister motif: Daisy's sister Julia provides Behler a carnal continuity with her family, even as Daisy's father Sam Moore practices incest with his eldest daughter, linking the family to Sinbad's lust. The incest theme is a Barthean favorite, appearing prominently in *Sot-Weed*, *Giles*, and *LETTERS*.

Reverberations past and present in Behler's life and correspondences among the long string of successive women from both eras are everywhere apparent. The metaphor for all these parallels and reflections is a can of Bon Ami Behler stole when he was in his early teens. The logo on the Bon Ami cans is a picture of a maid gazing at the endless reverberating reflections of herself as she stands between two mirrors. Behler has stolen the can, appropriating it for his own family's household use, but, reprimanded by his Aunt Rachel and ordered by his father to return it, he throws it into the creek. As he relates the tale to Daisy, she realizes, and causes him to see, that he is not a hero in the story, but a coward.

> When I was done she regarded me without expression for some moments....
> At last she said, "*You chickened out!*"
> "What do you mean?" But I knew already what she meant. Even as I was telling my story, I had seen myself for the first time from outside in, and was abashed at the sight. (*LV* 103)

The mirror image, by which Behler sees himself reflected in the eyes of a sympathetic woman, extends the mirror image on the Bon Ami can. Behler's women also mirror each other, and through his spiritual and physical intercourse with them Behler is at least partially able to clarify his own image. To underscore the Freudian complexities of his sibling relationship with Bijou, Behler has the habit of rocking in his sleep, even to the point of the violent gyrations that often accompany sex. His rocking back and forth not only suggests his continuing oscillation between two eras of time or segments of his own past, but also enables him, whether through interpretations of dreams or his own narratives, to come to know himself. Barth recently commented on Behler's need for self-knowledge: "I believe . . . that the dropout from the here and now, the Somebody character—who suffers from what I call ontological agnosticism—hasn't quite determined who he is."[2] Behler/Baylor's published stories—on topics like "Baylor in the Piazza San Marco" and "Baylor Jugged"—are one way of attempting to find himself in fiction. So, perhaps like Barth himself, he searches the Arabian past in an effort to find himself in the twentieth-century present.

Thus structure parallels events from Behler's twentieth-century youth and their mirror images in his Arabian adventures. The initiatory swim and the leaking boat, in which he becomes literally the bailer, both foreshadow events in the future. His lovemaking with Daisy on his sister's grave is destined to reverberate through his other affairs, all images of his original or imaginary love affair in the womb. The anger of his wife Jane over Behler's extramarital relations and his treatment of her reverberates through Jayda's account of her own trials as abused would-be wife, and Kurzia's bodily talent for artistic interpretation parallels the orgasmic and photographic inspirations of Julia, who, like her sister, collaborates with realistic images in the interpretations of Behler's Spanish sojourn and voyages. The images of most, if not all, of Behler's former lovers are manifested in Yasmin, who, like her counterparts Kurzia and Jayda, can assume the identities of others and serve as loving surrogates.

Together the sexual prowess of Behler's women reaches nearly supernatural proportions, first with the transformation of Behler from child to man by Daisy, and later by Jayda's remarkable ability to read the future in response to the phallic thrusts of Sinbad, practicing a kind of vaginal phrenology. If anything, *The Last Voyage* is a sexual allegory, dependent for its meaning and ultimate resolution on the question of Yasmin's virginity. At least twice broken by Behler and/or Sinbad and restored by Jayda's artifice, Yasmin's *virgo* is hardly *intacta*. In addition to daily involuntary anal intercourse with Behler, which keeps her reconstructed hymen ever fresh, Yasmin's worth goes up and down with the suitors' ebbing or increasing suspicions regarding her virginity. The theme has been used before by Barth in *Sot-Weed*, with the climactic deflowering of Pocahontas, and in *Giles Goat-Boy*, where the issue of doubtful parentage and virginity is one of those indecisive factors on which Giles's semi-divinity depends. As Barth so often reiterates, "The key to the treasure *is* the treasure."

The center of the climactic action is not bedroom but bathtub. Both are scenes of sexual encounter, but Sinbad's bathtub is not only his place of cohabitation, but also his ultimate escape mechanism, from both internal as well as external perils. He avoids blame for his misdeeds both by sailing away in his bathtub while others perish at sea, and by feigning madness in his lust, thus eliminating the need to marry his concubine, and then by feigning feigning madness in his attempt to commit incest with his daughter. The tub is the source of carnally linked meditations on the past, dark suspicions of the present, and predictions of the future. In that regard Sinbad's sexual repository bears more than a nominal relationship to Behler's adventures in Soper's Hole. The remaining unresolved question, regarding whether Sinbad has put the tub to incestuous use by deflowering his daughter—as Sam Moore deflowered Daisy—seems in the larger perspective of things almost insignificant.

Indeed, Barth's books seem almost a pageant of panegyrics to reproduction. *The Floating Opera*, *The End of the Road*, *Sot-Weed*, and *Giles* all involve the question of dubious parentage, and the "night-sea journey" by the tired but ultimately loving sperm in *Lost in the Funhouse* is complemented by a play in *Tidewater* involving egg-sisters floating down the tubes and meeting with their floating inseminators suspiciously like the floating canisters containing the play itself—found by the Sagamores and mated with their own stories to gestate ultimately into a novel of artistic reproduction. The reproductive topography of confluence (Y) is explained in *The Last Voyage* using Yasmin's as the inscribed body for the text:

> On his knees beside her in the dark he declared that there was another, better way to read that letter—a way that did not divide but rather merged us, as the Tigris and the Euphrates flow together into the Shatt al Arab and thence into the Persian Gulf. Moving her hand back down from her left breast toward her navel, he said, "Here is Yasmin, voyaging through her girlhood into her womanhood and surviving that rough passage." Leaving her hand there, he next moved his own from her right breast toward that same destination. "And here comes Somebody-or-Other, no sooner finding a self for himself than losing it or leaving it behind. At this point here—let's call it the Axis of the World—their separate voyages cast them together." (*LV* 366)

Behler's sexual metamorphosis image is, of course, another version of the contemporary novelist's seeking replenishment through innovative use of the literature of exhaustion. If his long love affair with Scheherazade results in still another modern offspring, it is one in which Barth continues increasingly to examine his own persona in terms of the way the parodist is also a dissembler. The ambiguous trickster figures of the earlier books, the black Doctor and Burlingame, metamorphose in later works into more sinister guises such as Bray and now Sinbad himself, who seem increasingly evil. As I have suggested, Barth through these trickster figures represents his own alter ego, a dark side of himself and the regenerative enterprise he is about. If my idea is right, then surely Sinbad is the same sort of alter ego for both Barth and Behler. Yet it is possible to share unsavory traits with a disreputable mirror-self without becoming a total blackguard. Sinbad is not totally condemned by the all-wise arbitrator of justice, Haroun Al Rachid. Sinbad is clever; he conceals his own moral and physical shortcomings; he is self-serving, even to the point of bloodthirstiness; and he is greedy and covetous. However, there is no reason that the modern hero closest to the author himself must be the complete rascal that his counterpart is, but merely that Behler exhibit some similar characteristics, and at the same time be unsure of his own identity and where his own mind is.

To aid his personal identity confusion, Behler is known by a number of different names: William Simon Behler, Simon, Simmon, Persimmon, Sy, William Baylor, Bill Baylor, Bey-el-Loor, Sinbad the Still Stranded, Sinbad the Landman, and Our Man. Behler is thus a bailer of leaking boats and a Bay-ler who sails the Chesapeake. Knowing Barth's affinity for music, one is tempted to add Bill Bailey, of "Bill Bailey, Won't You Please Come Home?"

Not all of Behler's name/identity changes are the result of other characters' coining original nomenclature for him. He writes under the pen name Baylor and tells just as much of his history at any time as suits his purpose. Prudent perhaps, but he is a professional verbal dissembler and not entirely an innocent. Barth tells us:

I believe, though, that the dropout from the here and now, the Somebody character—who suffers from what I call ontological agnosticism—hasn't quite determined who he is. He no doubt is losing a kind of innocence at the end, but in my view, retains what the Catholics would call a kind of remnant of invisible innocence right through. I think that's what saves him, as a matter of fact. And it's what would make him, to me, salvageable as a moral figure in the book.[3]

On the other hand, Sinbad the Sailor, like other trickster figures, seems to know who he is, even if, like Burlingame, he pretends to know all the answers but spends his life in the pursuit of his personal identity. One thing that Sinbad does recognize is that there is a similarity between himself and Behler. He makes this apparent in calling Behler Sinbad and referring to him as "my brother." At heart they are both consummate tale-tellers. Sinbad's tales, of course, come ultimately from Scheherazade, as do Behler's and Barth's. Yet, while the synopses Sinbad gives during his after-dinner sessions are cut short in Behler's account of them, they are not completely coincidental with Sir Richard Burton's version of the voyages, and we are led to believe that even before Behler has put his own spin on them, Sinbad is not telling them exactly as they appear in the Burton translation of *The Arabian Nights*. Since Scheherazade is the narrator in the second frame story, it is possible that she too did a variation on her own original stories, but Behler would have us believe that the principal changes, especially the wholly new and original elaborations and additions, are his own. We have to believe him, since he narrates the original frame story to his doctor, and thus has ultimate control over the yarns he spins, just as Barth controls everything Behler says.

Nevertheless, Behler's compulsion to tell his sister Bijou everything in his childhood directly leads to his compulsion to tell the female doctor everything at the end. The doctor, with the green eyes of Daisy and Yasmin, and with Bijou's apparent ability to listen, becomes a combination of all Behler's women, his major audience. Bijou begins listening in the womb; Daisy hears his youthful tribulations; Yasmin has listened to most of his story at least twice; Scheherazade must have heard it all from Behler somewhere; and Daisy's sister, Julia, has heard at least the first fifty-four years of the recital. Wives, daughters, and lovers blend into each other's common characteristics, and, except for Jane and possibly Bijou, finally into one mutually insatiable, ever-orgasmic entity.

The real treasure both Sinbad and Behler bring home from each of their successive voyages is the story of that voyage, but while Sinbad brings home new wealth each time, Behler brings home another idyllic memory of carnal abandon with an ever more desirable woman. The concluding story, "The Destroyer of Delights or The Familiar Stranger," reveals Behler's green-eyed doctor to be none other than his long-lost, dead sister, whose final beckoning to Behler to follow her out of the hospital/womb might indeed be a reenactment of his birth. Yet her eyes are the same color as Yasmin's, and if Yasmin is merely Behler's surrogate projection of sexual and spiritual fulfillment with his dead sister, the substitution raises a number of psychological possibilities and questions. Did Behler make up the entire tale as some sort of prenatal sexual wish fulfillment for relations with his own twin? Was Yasmin's final beckoning to Behler to follow her to the magic island simply a reenactment of Daisy's, or Bijou's, or even Julia's invitation, or did it provide both model and imitation? Is Behler still to be born, or born again in death, and if so will his new life take place in prewar Dorset or during Sinbad's last years? How did Scheherazade hear about Somebody the Sailor? Was the whole thing, including the frame in which she asks for her own death, her invention or Behler's? Who was whose invention, copy, approximation? Was the tale prenatal, or a Valkyrie's swan-song? Of course, in a way all the questions purposely raised by the frames, characters, and events are irrelevant, but Barth's old adage that the key to the treasure (its method of telling) is the treasure is partially belied by our fascination with the story itself, perhaps the best one Barth has yet told. Still, who can separate the story from its rendition? The frames with all their ambiguities of resolution are as much, if not a greater part of the story than individual events.

In *The Last Voyage* Barth blends frame complexity and self-reflexivity with characters' affinities and the similarities between past and present. In addition the reader should note not only the correspondence between Sinbad's and Behler's voyage stories, but also their relation to Burton's original translation of *The Arabian Nights*. Behler gives the reader his often synoptic version of Sinbad's tales, which in the main are fairly close to the original Burton version. Where the stories differ or are more elaborate than the original, more often than not the differences are especially significant. A prime example of Barth elaborating on Burton occurs in the tale of Sinbad's fifth voyage, where Burton's version has Sinbad deciding to take the repulsive Old Man of the Sea on his back in hope of heavenly reward: "I will deal kindly with him and do what he desireth; it may be I shall win me a reward in heaven for he may be a paralytic."[4] Barth's version involves Sinbad's identification and kinship with the old man:

> A closer look revealed my monster-designate to be just another castaway like myself, only older—*so* like myself, indeed, that when he turned his sea-seasoned face my way it was as if I looked into time's mirror and saw either my long-dead father or myself many voyages hence, wrapped head to toe in Experience's leafy lessons and grown so wise willy-nilly as to be rendered mute.... In that clear pool I saw me carrying myself ever deeper, step by step, until the human Sinbad who speaks words like these and behaves to man as man was all but submerged, and the blind old carving on his back—ageless, tireless, wordless but alas not toothless—had its way with that young vine. (*LV* 389)

Patricia Tobin has written an especially insightful study of Barth from the perspective of Harold Bloom's anxiety of influence.[5] Using Bloom's notion that certain writers operate constantly under the threat of merely copying their literary forebears and try to write against such anxiety, Tobin's study applies this neo-Freudian perspective convincingly to all Barth's fiction. While Tobin does not include the above passage in her examples, the quotation unmistakably indicates such an anxiety. Sinbad's carrying on his back the old man, with the disgusting and befouling weight of his omnivorous appetite and elimination—someone who, if he stays attached, will gradually destroy Sinbad—is a metaphor for the all-pervasive paternal influence which consumes its own offspring, and destroys the freedom and creativity of the writer. This allegorical danger is particularly acute for a writer like Barth, so cognizant of the literary past that everything he writes emerges in some sort of parody form, even as he strives to bring replenishment to his now exhausted literary predecessors.

Still another threat emerges from Barth's literary effort: the sacrifice of substance to form. No one is more aware than Barth himself of his own ingeniousness in applying new forms to old stories, or more freely or clearly calling self-reflexive attention to the problems of writing fiction that addresses such problems. As he has said, *The Last Voyage* retreats somewhat from the complexities that entangle narrative understanding in his earlier works.[6] Like Sinbad, who has to rid himself of the old man's stranglehold, Behler has to rid himself of Sinbad's and ultimately Scheherazade's overweening grip on the substance of the book's narrative. Hence they engage in a narrative competition, both caught in the grip of their ur-stories, and each building on the narrative framework developed by the other. As Sinbad puts it, "Awake and asleep we sail by turns two voyages, now parallel, now worlds apart, yet at times so close that the voyager may be transported unawares from one ship to the other" (*LV* 81).

In *The Last Voyage* as a whole Barth's regenerative contemporary imagination provides their escape by means of a new statement in which Sinbad grudgingly accepts the truth of his own actions and motivations, while Behler/Barth, who never gives up the present time—represented by his Seiko watch—reemerges in his own age with a new and different narrative to tell, just as Scheherazade wins her own peaceful place in the next world with a new story.

As Gregory Wolfe points out, Sinbad and Behler are mirror images of each other;[7] in *The Last Voyage* Sinbad's stories start out as allegories making ambiguous moral points (for example, "Men should behave to men as men") that often resemble the amoral proverbs of Barth's earlier books ("The key to the treasure is the treasure"). However, Sinbad emerges more corrupt and manipulative in each tale, until his aphorisms are replaced by the truths the other characters tell. Behler's stories are the opposite from self-aggrandizement in that he is far from heroic, even in the *Bildungsroman* section. Behler may behave badly sometimes, but he is always truthful. While Sinbad's guests see Somebody's stories as tedious and far-fetched (resembling the spectrum of anti-Barth critics in their criticism), the contemporary reader is increasingly led to regard Sinbad's stories as apocryphal, while Behler's seem honest, realistic, and truthful. Barth thus assumes the dual identities of an honest, modern story broker and an ancient, Harold Bray-like dissembler, who twists the old stories to his delightfully funny amoral purposes. Just as Sinbad recognizes his dark side in the Old Man on his back, so Barth must recognize the sinister ingeniousness and artifice that lend sophistication to his writing even as they diminish verisimilitude and mock philosophical guidance. In this readily understandable but hardly simplistic novel, the evidence of compositional struggle is as apparent as it was in the battle of father and son in "Bellerophoniad," or in the authorial struggles of *Lost in the Funhouse*.

Readers of *Somebody the Sailor* probably suspect that they have not heard the last of Scheherazade, nor of time-traveling between the modern Eastern Shore of Maryland and ancient Arabia. Even now, peacefully accompanying the "Destroyer of Delights," the ur-storyteller is not free from Barth's resurrection. Barth doesn't even need a Seiko to get her back. Most Timexes have the same buttons and knobs, and are much more easily acquired, simple to operate, and keep excellent time.

NOTES

1. Barth discussed the problems related to writing out of his own life experiences in an interview with Bin Ramke and Donald Revell in the *Bloomsbury*

Review 11 (October 1991): 3, 8. While maintaining his traditional distance from identifying his own life with that of any of his characters ("it would be a . . . dangerous game to come too close to the bone, in my own experience"), he speaks of the realist writer's need to alter and/or throw out of his own fiction those events and similarities which serve no artistic purpose, in much the same way Behler testifies to the liberties he has taken with his own experiences in his publications.

2. Ibid., p. 8.

3. Ibid.

4. Richard F. Burton, *The Book of the Thousand Nights and a Night*, vol. 6 (Burton Club Private Edition, n.d.), p. 51.

5. Patricia Tobin, *John Barth and the Anxiety of Continuance* (Philadelphia: University of Pennsylvania Press, 1992).

6. Ramke and Revell interview, p. 3.

7. Gregory Wolfe, "A Traveler's Tale," *The World and I* 6 (July 1991): 372.

Appendix 1: Selected List of Recurrent Themes, Patterns, and Techniques

BI-GENDERED COMPOSITION, OR JOINT AUTHORSHIP

A major theme in *Chimera*, *Sabbatical*, *The Tidewater Tales*, and *The Last Voyage of Somebody the Sailor*, the idea of bi-gendered composition grew from the swimming sperm in "Night-Sea Journey" looking for a mate. The motif continued through the rest of Barth's books, although used to a lesser extent in *LETTERS*, where Lady Amherst is as much sounding board as creator to her writer-lover Ambrose. The idea came into full fruition in the cooperation of the Genie and Scheherazade in "Dunyazadiad," *Tidewater*, and *The Last Voyage*, and developed in the husband-wife teams and couples in *Sabbatical* and *Tidewater*.

FEMINIST ISSUES

Barth was accused by some critics of his early books of maintaining a blatant sexism in his stereotyping of women as sex objects, a criticism he in part dispelled in depicting later female characters as strong creative forces both in resolving the dilemmas in which the male protagonists learn the truth about themselves, and in cooperating in the composition of the works in which the women appear. Germaine Amherst's epistles supply much of the continuity of *LETTERS*. Scheherazade, Barth's most self-reliant woman and his master storyteller, is more than coequal in "Dunyazadiad," and Susan Turner is a full if not quite equal partner in *Sabbatical*. Katherine Sagamore of *The Tidewater Tales* is a feminist from a matriarchal family, and Scheherazade returns to offer her invaluable service as storyteller to conclude that novel. In Barth's latest novel, *The*

Last Voyage of Somebody the Sailor, his burlesque depiction of Arabic insistence on bridal virginity is played out against a background of incestuous usurpation and modern feminist women.

HEROIC-MYTHIC PATTERNS

Joseph Campbell and Lord Raglan established that the heroes of literary antiquity all shared common aspects of origin and the circular pattern of their activities. When Barth was reminded by a critic that he had followed the traditional heroic cycles of Raglan and Campbell without realizing it in *Sot-Weed*, he began to capitalize on their explanations of the heroic pattern by parodying the cycles in *Giles* and *Chimera*, and adapting the cycles to other traditional literary behavior patterns such as the *Bildungsroman* and its artistic counterpart, the *Künstlerroman*.

MÖBIUS STRIP

Used as a structural metaphor for stories that circle back on themselves in one long continuum, the Möbius strip—one end of a strip of paper is rotated 180 degrees, then the ends are joined, creating a one-sided surface—begins *Lost in the Funhouse*, and then becomes Barth's image for repetition within and among his own tales and parodies of earlier canonical literature. Unlike the circle, in which the reader sees the same thing again and again in endless repetition, the Möbius strip, being twisted and folded back on itself, presents a new perspective every time the reader passes "go." Examples are the repeated trials and examinations Giles must undergo to fulfill his assignment sheet and proceed to graduation, each time coming to a different conclusion regarding what is "Passéd" and what "Flunkéd"; and the amphorae launched in the last *Funhouse* story, "Anonymiad," which become the sperm cells swimming up the tubes in the opening story, "Night-Sea Journey."

PARODY OR BURLESQUE

The techniques of parody or burlesque are major staples of all Barth's works, including the dark parodies of existentialism in *The Floating Opera* and *The End of the Road*; the literary parodies of eighteenth-century forms in *The Sot-Weed Factor* and *LETTERS*; the parodies of Greek antiquity in *Giles*, *Lost in the Funhouse*, and *Chimera*; the parodies of mythology and the heroic tradition in *Giles Goat-Boy* and *Chimera*; the parodies of *The Arabian Nights* in *Chimera*, *The Tidewater Tales*, and *The Last Voyage of*

Somebody the Sailor; and the parodies of American life and literature in *The Sot-Weed Factor*, *Giles Goat-Boy*, and *Sabbatical*, to name only a few. In all of these, Barth's comedy springs from an inventive use of contemporary slang and idiosyncratic language, and the imposition of modern skepticism to debunk the hallowed traditions of the past. I do not mean to imply that every work is limited to only one parody or type of parody, or even multi-parodies of a single era or idea. Nearly all Barth's works are rife with all manner of parodies, often exaggerated to burlesque form. The technique is Barth's principal means of enhancing traditional forms through comic updating.

SELF-REFLEXIVITY

The term *self-reflexivity* might loosely be defined as Barth's discussing himself or the author's role in creating the novel or story in which the discussion takes place. This tendency permeates all Barth's work either directly or indirectly. Each of his surface plots has either a direct or indirect analogue in the problems of writing. In a number of instances—notably many of the stories in *Lost in the Funhouse*, two of the three novellas of *Chimera*, *Sabbatical*, *The Tidewater Tales*, and *The Last Voyage of Somebody the Sailor*—the principal dilemma involves how to recount the events successfully rather than how to overcome any obstacles the events themselves impose. The motif ranges from the psychotherapy of recording the events of one's life, through the protagonist/writer's trying to overcome writer's block, to the quest for a way to retell an old story in a new way.

SEX AND REPRODUCTION

All of Barth's works involve sexual encounters, and the problems of his characters stem largely from libidinous impulses and sexual attraction. It is not that his books merely have a lot of sex in them; instead, sex becomes the key to the questions raised by the books. For instance, the method of Pocahontas's deflowering in *The Sot-Weed Factor* and the question of Yasmin's virginity in *The Last Voyage of Somebody the Sailor* are the principal—if comic—issues of the respective plots. Barth's fourth book, *Giles Goat-Boy*, represents a milestone in which sex becomes for the first time a part of the solution (mutually orgasmic coition) to the protagonist's dilemma, a theme that is—with the exception of *LETTERS*—continued throughout Barth's works. Sex and reproduction become metaphors for artistic creativity or the production of new fiction in "Night-Sea Journey,"

Sabbatical, and *The Tidewater Tales*, and a way of reading both the past and the future in *The Last Voyage of Somebody the Sailor*.

TRICKSTER FIGURES

In his books Barth utilizes the mythic trickster figure, a character of ambiguous morality and one who may or may not have contact with or be imbued with supernatural powers. The figure is chameleon in the sense of being able to adopt a number of disguises or identities, about the authenticity of any of which even the protagonist is in doubt. Tricksters are traditionally boundary violators, linking them to the protagonist/writer/author, who is also attempting to violate the boundaries of traditional literature. Thus tricksters provide a dark alter ego to the protagonist/writer, the most notable being Bray in *Giles Goat-Boy* and *LETTERS*, Burlingame in *The Sot-Weed Factor*, Polyeidus in "Bellerophoniad," and Sinbad in *The Last Voyage of Somebody the Sailor*.

TWINNING

The term *"twinning"* originated with Barth, and is used extensively by critics to describe Barth's tendency to produce books in pairs in order to present two different aspects of a single problem or plot situation. The most notable examples of "twinned" books are *The Floating Opera* and *The End of the Road*, representing different aspects of existential philosophy, and *Sabbatical* and *The Tidewater Tales*, as joint marital coauthorship ventures in overcoming writer's block.

Twinning also applies to the literal sets of twins in Barth's works. In the case of the fraternal male-female twins such as Eben and Anna in *Sot-Weed* and Behler and Bijou in *Somebody*, there are overtly incestuous overtones to the relationships, while twins of the same sex usually imply sibling rivalry and manifestations of alter-ego behavior, as in the nameless Siamese twin brothers of "Petition" as well as Mims and Susan and Manfred and Peter of *Sabbatical*. Barth pushes his own twins motif to the point of burlesque in *Tidewater*, when the Sagamores try out dozens of "funny pairs of girl-and-boy names like Arts and Sciences and Wash and Wear and Renaissance and Reformation" (*TWT* 479), emphasizing the duality of existence and our own pattern of binary reasoning.

Barth's twinning extends also to his pairing of characters. *Chimera*, for example, pairs Perseus and Bellerophon; *Giles*, the Rexford brothers; *Sot-Weed*, Burlingame and Billy Rumbly; and *Somebody*, Behler and Sinbad, among the scores of pairings found throughout Barth's works. Complementary characters emphasize different aspects of a basic mental predisposition, or force comparisons between seemingly diverse characters.

UNRELIABLE NARRATORS

Although the narrator-characters of *The Floating Opera*, *The End of the Road*, and *The Sot-Weed Factor* often have skewed judgment, Barth's introductory and concluding material in *Giles Goat-Boy* purposely calls into question both the authenticity and the narrator's point of view and his (its) motivation for creating the *Revised New Syllabus*. Just who is narrating "Bellerophoniad" is also a principal question in *Chimera*, while the historical accounts of shape-changing A. B. Cook IV and Jerome Bray in *LETTERS* are scarcely intended to be swallowed whole by the reader.

Just as Barth warns us that the fiction he produced is not his own story, so we must be on guard against the authors-within-the-stories who claim to be telling the truth of their own histories. One of Barth's most reliable narrators—Behler, of *The Last Voyage of Somebody the Sailor*—admits to altering his account of Sinbad's retelling of his own voyages, leading us to be always skeptical of whether anyone's account in Barth's works is totally unbiased.

VOYAGES

All of Barth's books except *The End of the Road* and *Giles Goat-Boy* contain or detail voyages across water. Beginning with the fantasy voyage of the barge *The Floating Opera* past an imaginary crowd of readers, Barth's voyages are trips into adventure, romance, despair, and creativity. As a whole they share much with Sinbad's voyages in that the author/protagonist returns each time with the treasure of a new tale or an old story replenished. Barth's last four novels are principally voyage stories rather than tales with incidental voyages. Certainly his preoccupation with sailing is due to the locale in and of which he writes as uncrowned Poet Laureate of the Chesapeake Bay.

WATER-MESSAGES

Floating messages in a bottle and amphorae, bearing cryptic noninformation in "Water-Message" and the entire personal history of the minstrel in "Anonymiad," are complemented later by Mack's floating freeze-dried turd and Paisley's empty boat in *LETTERS*, and the canisters containing the play SEX EDUCATION, set adrift in *Sabbatical* and resurrected in *The*

Tidewater Tales. The water-messages, still undecipherable by the young surrogate-author Ambrose at the beginning of Barth's career, come to be metaphors of artistic inspiration as his voice and accomplishment develop.

Appendix 2: Biographical Note on John Barth

John Simmons Barth was born to John Jacob and Georgia (Simmons) Barth on May 27, 1930 in Cambridge, Maryland. After graduating from high school, Barth briefly attended the Julliard School of Music before enrolling as a scholarship student at Johns Hopkins University. While an undergraduate, he published two stories in the student literary magazine and "Lilith and the Lion" in the *Hopkins Review*. He married Harriette Anne Strickland on January 11, 1950. He received his B.A. in creative writing from Hopkins and enrolled in the institution's graduate writing program in 1951—the same year his daughter Christine was born. The next year he completed his M.A. thesis, "Shirt of Nessus" and began work on the doctorate.

After the birth of his son John in 1952, Barth had to leave graduate school for financial reasons. He accepted a position as an instructor in the English Department at Pennsylvania State University in 1953, and the next year saw the birth of his second son, Daniel. Barth spent the first three months of 1955 writing the first part of *The Floating Opera*, the next three months revising it for his publisher, and the last three months of the year writing *The End of the Road*.

After *The End of the Road* was published and nominated for the National Book Award, Barth was promoted to Assistant Professor. He was already at work on *The Sot-Weed Factor*, which was ultimately published in 1960 and followed by a promotion to Associate Professor. In 1965 he accepted a position as Professor of English at the State University of New York at Buffalo. The next year *Giles Goat-Boy* was published, followed a year later by "The Literature of Exhaustion" in *Atlantic*, and revised editions of his first three books.

Lost in the Funhouse was published in 1968 and two years later Barth was appointed Edward H. Butler Professor of English at Buffalo. He was divorced in 1969 and married Shelly Rosenberg in 1970. He published *Chimera* in 1972 and the next year returned to Johns Hopkins as Alumni Centennial Professor of English and Creative Writing, dividing his time between Baltimore and his home on the Eastern Shore of Maryland.

Ten years of writing and research culminated in the publication of *LETTERS* in 1979, followed by the twin novels *Sabbatical* in 1982 and *The Tidewater Tales* in 1987. Barth's last major work of fiction to appear as of this writing is *The Last Voyage of Somebody the Sailor*, published in 1991.

His much debated "The Literature of Exhaustion" essay was followed thirteen years later, in 1980, by "The Literature of Replenishment"—clarifying, modifying, and updating his thinking regarding postmodern literature. A collection of his essays, including the previous two, was published in 1984 under the title, *The Friday Book: Essays and Other Nonfiction*.

Barth's awards and honors include National Book Award nominations for *The Floating Opera* and *Lost in the Funhouse*, and the Award itself for *Chimera*. He also won a Brandeis University Creative Arts Award in 1965, a Rockefeller Foundation grant for 1965–66, a National Institute of Arts and Letters grant in 1966, and an honorary Litt.D. degree from Johns Hopkins in 1973.

Selected Bibliography

BOOKS ON BARTH

Fogel, Stan, and Gordon Slethaug. *Understanding John Barth*. Columbia: University of South Carolina Press, 1990.
Harris, Charles B. *Passionate Virtuosity: The Fiction of John Barth*. Urbana: University of Illinois Press, 1983.
Morrell, David. *John Barth: An Introduction*. University Park: Pennsylvania State University Press, 1976.
Schulz, Max F. *The Muses of John Barth: Tradition and Metafiction from "Lost in the Funhouse" to "The Tidewater Tales."* Baltimore: Johns Hopkins University Press, 1990.
Tharpe, Jac. *John Barth: The Comic Sublimity of Paradox*. Carbondale: Southern Illinois University Press, 1974.
Tobin, Patricia. *John Barth and the Anxiety of Continuance*. Philadelphia: University of Pennsylvania Press, 1992.
Waldmeir, Joseph J., ed. *Critical Essays on John Barth*. Boston: G. K. Hall, 1980.
Walkiewicz, E. P. *John Barth*. Boston: G. K. Hall, 1986.
Ziegler, Heide. *John Barth*. London: Methuen, 1987.

BIBLIOGRAPHIES

Vine, Richard Allan. *John Barth: An Annotated Bibliography*. Metuchen, N.J.: Scarecrow Press, 1977.
Weixlmann, Joseph. "John Barth." In *American Novelists*. Contemporary Authors: Bibliographical Series 1. Edited by James J. Martine. Detroit: Gale, 1986, pp. 43–81.

———. *John Barth: A Descriptive Primary and Annotated Secondary Bibliography, Including a Descriptive Catalogue of Manuscript Holdings in United States Libraries*. New York: Garland, 1976.

GENERAL ARTICLES

Bradbury, John M. "Absurd Insurrection: The Barth-Percy Affair." *South Atlantic Quarterly* 68, no. 3 (1969): 319–29.

Dahiya, Bhim. "Structural Patterns in the Novels of Barth, Vonnegut and Pynchon." *Indian Journal of American Studies* 5 (1975): 53–68.

Davis, Robert Con. "The Case for a Post-Structuralist Mimesis: John Barth and Imitation." *American Journal of Semiotics* 3, no. 3 (1985): 49–72.

Farwell, Harold. "John Barth's Tenuous Affirmation: 'The Absurd, Unending Possibility of Love.' " *Georgia Review* 28, no. 2 (Summer 1974): 290–306.

Hafrey, Leigh. "The Gilded Cage: Postmodernism and Beyond." *Tri-Quarterly* 56 (Winter 1983): 126–36.

Harris, Charles B. "John Barth and the Critics: An Overview." *Mississippi Quarterly* 32, no. 2 (Spring 1979): 269–83.

Janoff, Bruce. "Black Humor, Existentialism, and Absurdity: A Generic Confusion." *Arizona Quarterly* 30 (1974): 293–304.

Johnstone, Douglas B. "John Barth and the Healing of the Self." *Mosaic* 21, no. 1 (Winter 1988): 67–78.

Kennard, Jean E. "John Barth: Imitations of Imitations." *Mosaic* 3 (Winter 1970): 116–31.

Klinkowitz, Jerome. "John Barth Reconsidered." *Partisan Review* 49, no. 3 (1982): 407–11.

Kostelanetz, Richard. " 'New American Fiction' Reconsidered." *TriQuarterly* 8 (1967): 279–86.

Margolies, Edward. "John Barth and the Barbarities of History." In *American Literature in Belgium*. Edited by Gilbert Debusscher. Amsterdam: Rodop, 1988, pp. 205–11.

Matthews, John T. "Intertextual Frameworks: The Ideology of Parody in John Barth." In *Intertextuality and Contemporary American Fiction*. Edited by Patrick O'Donnell and Robert Davis. Baltimore: Johns Hopkins University Press, 1989, pp. 35–57.

Safer, Elaine B. "The Essay as Aesthetic Mirror: John Barth's 'Exhaustion' and 'Replenishment.' " *Studies in American Fiction* 15, no. 1 (Spring 1987): 109–17.

Slethaug, Gordon E. "Barth's Refutation of the Idea of Progress." *Critique* 13, no. 3 (1971): 11–29.

Stubbs, John C. "John Barth as a Novelist of Ideas: The Themes of Value and Identity." *Critique* 8, no. 2 (Winter 1965–66): 101–16.

Tanner, Tony. "What Is the Case?" Chapter 10 of *City of Words: American Fiction 1950–1970*. London: Jonathan Cape, 1971, pp. 230–59.

Tatham, Campbell. "John Barth and the Aesthetics of Artifice." *Contemporary Literature* 12 (1971): 60–73.
Trachtenberg, Alan. "Barth and Hawkes: Two Fabulists." *Critique* 6, no. 2 (Fall 1963): 4–18.
Zamora, Lois Parkinson. "The Structural Games in the Fiction of John Barth and Julio Cortazar." *Perspectives on Contemporary Literature* 6 (1980): 28–36.

CRITICAL ESSAYS AND CHAPTERS ON INDIVIDUAL WORKS

The Floating Opera

Bluestone, George. "John Wain and John Barth: The Angry and the Accurate." *Massachusetts Review* 1 (Spring 1968): 582–89.
Kurk, Katherine C. "Narration as Salvation: Textual Ethics of Michel Tournier and John Barth." *Comparative Literature Studies* 25, no. 3 (1988): 251–62.
Le Clair, Thomas. "John Barth's *The Floating Opera*: Death and the Craft of Fiction." *Texas Studies in Literature and Language* 14, no. 4 (Winter 1973): 711–30.
Schickel, Richard. "*The Floating Opera*." *Critique* 6, no. 2 (Fall 1963): 53–67.

The End of the Road

Graff, Gerald E. "Mythotherapy and Modern Poetics." *TriQuarterly* 11 (1968): 76–90.
Kerner, David. "Psychodrama in Eden." *Chicago Review* 13 (Winter-Spring 1959): 59–67.
Majdiak, Daniel. "Barth and the Representation of Life." *Criticism* 12 (1970): 51–67.
Safer, Elaine. "John Barth, the University, and the Absurd: A Study of *The End of the Road* and *Giles Goat-Boy*." In *The American Writer and the University*. Edited by Ben Siegel. Newark: University of Delaware Press, 1989, pp. 88–100.
Smith, Herbert F. "Barth's Endless Road." *Critique* 6, no. 2 (Fall 1963): 68–76.

The Sot-Weed Factor

Betts, Richard A. "The Joke as Informing Principle in *The Sot-Weed Factor*." *College Literature* 10, no. 1 (1983): 38–49.
Dippie, Brian. " 'His Visage Wild; His Form Exotick': Indian Themes and Cultural Guilt in John Barth's *The Sot-Weed Factor*." *American Quarterly* 21 (1969): 113–21.
Diser, Philip. "The Historical Ebenezer Cooke." *Critique* 10, no. 3 (1968): 48–59.

Fiedler, Leslie. "John Barth: An Eccentric Genius." In *On Contemporary Literature*. Edited by Richard Kostelanetz. New York: Avon Books, 1964, pp. 238–43.
Gillespie, Gerald. "From 'Baroque' Michael Drayton to 'Enlightened' Ebenezer Cooke: (Re-)Debunking the American Golden Age." In *Erkennen und Deuten: Essays zur Literatur und Literaturtheorie Edgar Lohner in memoriam*. Edited by Martha Woodmansee and Walter F.W. Lohnes. Berlin: Erich Schmidt Verlag, 1983, pp. 326–34.
Gladsky, Thomas S. "*The Sot-Weed Factor* as Historiography." *Arkansas Philological Association* 7, no. 2 (1981): 37–47.
Gross, Beverly. "The Anti-Novels of John Barth." *Chicago Review* 20 (November 1968): 95–109.
Holder, Alan. " 'What Marvelous Plot . . . Was Afoot?' History in Barth's *The Sot-Weed Factor*." *American Quarterly* 20 (1968): 596–604.
Kostelanetz, Richard. *The New American Arts*. New York: Horizon Press, 1965, pp. 202–13.
Lee, L. L. "Some Uses of *Finnegans Wake* in John Barth's *The Sot-Weed Factor*." *James Joyce Quarterly* 5 (Winter 1968): 177–78.
Malloy, Jeanne M. "William Byrd's Histories and John Barth's *The Sot-Weed Factor*." *Mississippi Quarterly* 42, no. 2 (Spring 1989): 160–72.
Miller, Russell H. "*The Sot-Weed Factor*: A Contemporary Mock-Epic." *Critique: Studies in Modern Fiction* 8, no. 2 (Winter 1965–1966): 88–100.
Puetz, Manfred. "John Barth's *The Sot-Weed Factor*: The Pitfalls of Mythopoesis." In *Critical Essays on John Barth*. Edited by Joseph J. Waldmeir. Boston: G. K. Hall, 1980, pp. 134–45.
Rovit, Earl. "The Novel as Parody: John Barth." *Critique* 6, no. 2 (Fall 1963): 77–85.
Safer, Elaine. "The Allusive Mode and Black Humor in Barth's *Sot-Weed Factor*." *Studies in the Novel* 13 (1981): 424–38.
Sutcliffe, Denham. "Worth a Guilty Conscience." *Kenyon Review* 23 (1961): 181–84.
Winston, Robert P. "Chaucer's Influence on Barth's *The Sot-Weed Factor*." *American Literature* 56, no. 4 (December 1984): 584–90.

Giles Goat-Boy

Brooks, Peter. "John Barth." *Encounter* 28 (June 1967): 71–75.
Byrd, Scott. "*Giles Goat-Boy* Visited." *Critique* 9, no. 1 (1966): 108–12.
Gross, Beverly. "The Anti-Novels of John Barth." *Chicago Review* 20, no. 3 (November 1968): 95–109.
Jones, Deborah. "The Paradox of the Transcendental Trope: Intertextuality, or The Allegory of *Giles Goat-Boy*." *Southern Review* 20, no. 3 (1987): 240–60.
Jones, Fiona K. "The Twentieth Century Writer and the Image of the Computer." In *Computers and Human Communication: Problems and Prospects*. Edited by David L. Crowner and Laurence A. Marschall. Washington, D.C.: University Press of America, 1979, pp. 167–80.

Malvern, Marjorie M. "The Parody of Medieval Saints' Lives in John Barth's *Giles Goat-Boy, or The Revised New Syllabus*." *Studies in Medievalism* 2, no. 1 (Fall 1982): 59–76.
McDonald, James. "Barth's Syllabus: The Frame of *Giles Goat-Boy*." *Critique* 13, no. 3 (1971): 5–10.
Mercer, Peter. "The Rhetoric of *Giles Goat-Boy*." *Novel: A Forum on Fiction* 4 (Winter 1971): 147–58.
Tatham, Campbell. "The Gilesean Monomyth: Some Remarks on the Structure of *Giles Goat-Boy*." *Genre* 3 (December 1970): 364–75.
Tilton, John W. "*Giles Goat-Boy*: An Interpretation." *Bucknell Review* 18, no. 1 (1970): 92–119.

Lost in the Funhouse

Bell, Steven M. "Literature, Self-Consciousness, and Writing: The Example of Barth's *Lost in the Funhouse*." *International Fiction Review* 11, no. 2 (Summer 1984): 84–89.
Bienstock, Beverly Gray. "Lingering on the Autognostic Verge: John Barth's *Lost in the Funhouse*." *Modern Fiction Studies* 19, no. 1 (1973): 69–78.
Gillespie, Gerald. "Barth's *Lost in the Funhouse*: Short Story Text in Its Cyclic Context." *Studies in Short Fiction* 12 (1975): 223–30.
Kiernan, Robert F. "John Barth's Artist in the Fun House." *Studies in Short Fiction* 10, no. 4 (1973): 373–80.
Knapp, Edgar H. "Found in the Barthhouse: Novelist as Savior." *Modern Fiction Studies* 14 (Winter): 446–51.
Koelb, Clayton. "John Barth's 'Glossolalia.'" *Comparative Literature* 26, no. 3 (Summer 1974): 334–45.
Krier, William J. "*Lost in the Funhouse*: 'A Continuing, Strange Love Letter.'" *Boundary 2* 5 (1976): 103–16.
Malmgren, Carl D. "Modernist Postmodernist *Kunstlerroman*." *Novel: A Forum on Fiction* 21 (Fall 1987): 5–28.
Marta, Jan. "John Barth's Portrait on the Artist as a Fiction: Modernism Through the Looking-Glass." *Canadian Review of Contemporary Literature* 9 (June 1982): 208–22.
Rackham, Jeff. "John Barth's Four-and-Twenty Golden Umbrellas." *Midwest Quarterly* 22, no. 2 (Winter 1981): 163–75.
Shloss, Carol, and Khachig Tololyan. "The Siren in the Funhouse: Barth's Courting of the Reader." *Journal of Narrative Technique* 11, no. 1 (Winter 1981): 64–74.
Slaughter, Carolyn Norman. "Who Gets Lost in the Funhouse?" *Arizona Quarterly* 44, no. 4 (Winter 1989): 80–97.
Tanner, Tony. "No Exit." *Partisan Review* 36 (Spring 1969): 293–95, 297–99.
Tatham, Campbell. "Anima Rising: Notes Toward a Mediating Fiction." Paper presented at Modern Language Association, New York, December 1976.

Vitanza, Victor J. "The Novelist as Topologist: John Barth's *Lost in the Funhouse*." *Texas Studies in Language and Literature* 19, no. 1 (1977): 83–97.

Westervelt, Linda A. "Teller, Tale, Told: Relationships in John Barth's Latest Fiction." *Journal of Narrative Technique* 8, no. 1 (Winter 1978): 42–55.

Chimera

Edelstein, Marilyn. "The Function of Self-Consciousness in John Barth's *Chimera*." *Studies in American Fiction* 12, no. 1 (Spring 1984): 99–108.

Raper, Julius Rowan. "John Barth's *Chimera*: Men and Women under the Myth." *Southern Literary Journal* 22, no. 1 (Fall 1989): 17–31.

Wooley, Deborah Anne. "Erotic Dialogue, Impotent Monologue: Voices and Power in Barth's *Chimera*." Chapter 3 of *The Power to Tell: Narrative Voice in Self-Reflexive Fiction*. Seattle: University of Washington, 1981, pp. 134–61.

Ziegler, Heide. "A Room of One's Own: The Author and the Reader in the Text." In *Critical Angles: European Views of Contemporary American Literature*. Edited by Marc Chenetier. Carbondale: Southern Illinois University Press, 1986, pp. 45–59.

———. "The Tale of the Author or, Scheherazade's Betrayal." *Review of Contemporary Fiction* 10, no. 2 (Summer 1990): 82–88.

LETTERS

D'Haen, Theo. *Text to Reader: A Communicative Approach to Fowles, Barth, Cortázar and Boon*. Amsterdam: John Benjamins, 1983, pp. 43–68.

Graff, Gerald. "Under Our Belt and Off Our Back: Barth's *LETTERS* and Postmodern Fiction." *TriQuarterly* 52 (Fall 1981): 150–64.

McCaffery, Larry. "Barth's *LETTERS* and the Literature of Replenishment." *Chicago Review* 31, no. 4 (1980): 75–82.

Olster, Stacey. "John Barth: Clio as Kin to Calliope." Chapter 4 of *Reminiscence and Re-creation in Contemporary American Fiction*. Cambridge, Eng.: Cambridge University Press, 1989, pp. 106–36.

Robbins, Deborah J. "Whatever Happened to Realism? John Barth's *LETTERS*." *Northwest Review* 19, no. 1–2 (1981): 218–27.

Roemer, Marjorie Godlin. "The Paradigmatic Mind: John Barth's *LETTERS*." *Twentieth Century Literature* 33, no. 1 (Spring 1987): 38–50.

Schulz, Max F. "Barth, *LETTERS*, and the Great Tradition." *Genre* 14, no. 1 (Spring 1981): 95–115.

Shipe, Timothy. "A Note on *LETTERS*: *Poltroons and Patriots* and the "Posthumous" Letters of A. B. Cook IV." *Notes on Contemporary Literature* 10, no. 4 (1979): 11.

Stonehill, Brian. "A Trestle of *LETTERS*." Chapter 8 of *The Self-Conscious Novel: Artifice in Fiction from Joyce to Pynchon*. Philadelphia: University of Pennsylvania Press, 1988, pp. 157–67.
Strehle, Susan. "*LETTERS* and the Relative Frame." In *Fiction in the Quantum Universe*. Chapel Hill: University of North Carolina Press, 1992, pp. 124–58.
Thompson, Gary. "Barth's *LETTERS* and Hawkes' Passion." *Michigan Quarterly Review* 19 (1980): 270–78.

Sabbatical and *The Tidewater Tales*

Elliot, Emory. "History and Will in *Dog Soldiers*, *Sabbatical*, and *The Color Purple*." *Arizona Quarterly* 43 (Autumn 1988): 197–217.
Greer, Creed. "Abortion Stories: The Sexual Metaphorics of Organizing Barth's Texts." *Review of Contemporary Fiction* 10, no. 2 (1990): 76–81.
Harris, Charles B. "The Age of the World View: The Critique of Realism in John Barth's *Sabbatical*." In *Germany and German Thought in American Literature and Cultural Criticism*. Edited by Peter Freese. Essen: Verlag die Blaue, 1990, pp. 407–32.
Slethaug, Gordon E. "Floating Signifiers in John Barth's *Sabbatical*." *Modern Fiction Studies* 33, no. 4 (Winter 1987): 647–55.
Weiser, Irwin. "Barth's *Sabbatical*." *Explicator* 42, no. 2 (Winter 1984): 22–23.

The Last Voyage of Somebody the Sailor

Edmundson, Mark. "The End of the Road." *New Republic* 204 (April 22, 1991): 43–46.
Flower, Dean. "Not Waving but Drowning." *Hudson Review* 44 (Summer 1991): 317.
Gromer, Crystal. "Sinbad the Sailor II." *Commonweal* 118 (May 17, 1991): 341.
Harrison, M. John. "Adrift on a Sea of Stories." *Times Literary Supplement*, November 15, 1991, p. 7.
Raban, Jonathan. "The Sloop of Araby." *New York Times Book Review*, February 3, 1991, p. 3.
Wolfe, Gregory. "A Traveler's Tale." *World and I* 6 (July 1991): 371–75.

NONFICTION WRITINGS BY BARTH

Barth, John. *The Friday Book: Essays and Other Nonfiction*. New York: G. P. Putnam's Sons, 1984.
———. "Teacher: The Making of a Good One." *Harper's* 273 (November 1986): 58–65.
———. "Welcome to College—and My Books." *New York Times Book Review*, September 16, 1984, pp. 1, 36–37.

INTERVIEWS

Enck, John J. "John Barth: An Interview." *Wisconsin Studies in Contemporary Literature* 6 (Winter-Spring 1965): 3–14.

Howell, John, ed. "John Barth." Introduction by Sarah Zimmerman. *Papyrus* 1 (Spring 1987): 39–49.

Lampkin, Loretta M. "An Interview with John Barth." *Contemporary Literature* 29, no. 4 (1988): 485–97.

Ramke, Bin, and Donald Revell. "Conversation with Prime Maximalist John Barth." *Bloomsbury Review* 11 (October 1991): 3, 8.

Reilly, Charlie. "An Interview with John Barth." *Contemporary Literature* 22, no. 1 (1981): 1–23.

Index

Absalom! Absalom!, 103
The Aeneid, 74
Alter, Robert, 110
American Antiquarian Society, 22
Anchor Doubleday, 35, 101
Appleton-Century-Crofts, 13, 101
The Arabian Nights, 121, 125, 126–27

Bakhtin, Mikhail, 36
Barth, John Simmons: awards by, 138; biographical note on, 137–38; credibility of narrators and, 135; feminism and, 131–32; heroic patterns and, 132; humor of, xi; incest theme and, 121; joint-authorship motif by, 131; literary criticism by, xi-xii; literary criticism of, xii-xiv; literary imitation by, 127; Mobius strip motif by, 132; parodies by, 132–33; passionate virtuosity of, 113; plot replication by, 13; quoted on sexual metaphors, 99; reproductive theme by, 123–24; resiliency of, xi; self-reflexivity by, xi, 133; sexual rivalry and, 25; sexual themes by, 133–34; trickster figures and, 134; twinning by, 134–35; voyage motif by, 119, 135; water-messages and, 135–36. *See also names of specific works*
Barth, Shelley, 99, 138
Bloom, Harold, xiii, 127
Burton, Richard, 125, 126

Campbell, Joseph, 35, 36, 72, 73, 132
Candide, 18
Chimera: character development in, 68; gender equality and, 70–71, 72; heroic patterns in, 72–74, 76–77; language traits of, 77; male-female authorship and, 99; narrative patterns of, 68; narrator's challenge and, 67–68; "plot" of, 68; reality and, 77–78; recapitulation in, 75; self-reflexivity in, 69, 74, 75–76; sexuality in, 69, 71; sexual role changes and, 71–72; *The Tidewater Tales* and, 112, 117; time aspect and, 76–77
Conroy, Gabriel, 51, 52
Cooke, Ebenezer, 21–22, 23, 24, 31
The Country Wife, 14

Davis, Cynthia, 75
The Divine Comedy, 45

Dubliners, 51–52

Edelstein, Marilyn, 68
Eliot, T. S., 92, 93, 94, 95, 106
Ellmann, Richard, 62
The End of the Road: allegorical cast of, 17–18; comic aspects of, 14; existentialism in, 19; *The Floating Opera* and, 13–14, 100; irrationality and, 15–16; mythotherapy and, 15; name significance in, 14; nihilism and, 13–14, 15; publishing of, 101; satiric parodies in, 17; scriptotherapy and, 15, 16; sexuality in, 16–17; *The Sot-Weed Factor* and, 26–27

Fawcett Columbine, 101
Fiedler, Leslie, 23
Fielding, Henry, 21, 24
Film, 95–96
Finnegans Wake, 110
"The Fire Sermon," 94
The Floating Opera: absurdity in, 5–7, 9; audience comprehension and, 1; Barth's future works and, 8; climax of, 10–11; comic aspects of, 9–10; emotional moments theory and, 4–5; *The End of the Road* and, 13–14, 100; existentialism and, 2, 4, 7, 8–9, 11; fear and, 4; *The Good Soldier* and, 1; metaphoric structure of, 2–4, 7, 8; name significance in, 14; narrative emphasis of, 8; nihilism and, 13; personal vs. social obligation and, 2–3; publishing of, 101; sexuality in, 9; suspense of, 2; *Tristram Shandy* and, 2
Fogel, Stan, xiii
Ford, Ford Maddox, 1
Freud, Sigmund, 40
The Friday Book, xi-xii, 35

Gabler, Hans, 62

Giles Goat-Boy: character analogies in, 42–44; character opposition and, 44–45; comic nature of, 35–36, 39–40; credibility and, 84; frame paraphernalia of, 47–48; heroic patterns in, 35, 36, 38–39, 40–42, 73; literary imitation in, 35, 45, 48; metaphors in, 42; popularity of, 42; religious symbolism in, 39, 40–41, 46–47; self-reflexivity and, 48–49; sexuality and, 46, 123; *The Sot-Weed Factor* and, 27; time element and, 39, 42
Gillespie, Gerald, 57
The Good Soldier, 1
Graff, Gerald, 90
Graves, Robert, 73, 77–78
The Great Gatsby, 18
Gross, Beverly, 48
Gulliver's Travels, 47

Harris, Charles, xiii, 17, 24, 52, 70, 82, 113
Heidegger, Martin, 14
Helen in Egypt, 62
The Hero, 35
The Hero with a Thousand Faces, 35
Hopkins Review, 137

Inquiry, 5
Ireland, 22–23

John Barth and the Anxiety of Continuance, xiii
John Barth: An Introduction, xiii
Johns Hopkins University, 137, 138
Joyce, James, 22, 51–52, 63
Julliard School of Music, 137

Krier, William J., 62, 63
Kudove, 106

The Last Voyage of Somebody the Sailor: *The Arabian Nights* and, 126–27; frame narrative of, 120;

mirror image in, 122–23, 128; name identity changes and, 124–25; *The 1001 Nights* and, 119–20; self-reflexivity and, 120, 124, 126; as sexual allegory, 123–24; sister motif in, 121

LETTERS: anticipation device in, 84; artistic aspect of, 95–97; audience demand and, 81; chronological framework of, 82–83, 88; credibility and, 84–85, 87–88; historical aspect of, 82–92; literary status of, 81; male-female authorship motif and, 99; number significance in, 82–83, 84; postmodern fiction and, 90; sex-as-inspiration idea and, 99; societal problems and, 113; *The Tidewater Tales* and, 115; title explanation of, 82; treatment of women in, 92–94; water-messages in, 89–90

"The Literature of Exhaustion," xii

"The Literature of Replenishment," xii

Lost in the Funhouse: Barth's existential despair and, 59; bizarre metaphors in, 58–59; *Dubliners* and, 51–52; heroic patterns in, 73; love and, 62–63; male-female authorship motif and, 99, 101; narcissistic dilemma of, 60; narrator protagonist of, 52–53; *The Odyssey* and, 61–62; recapitulation and, 63–64; religious irony in, 59; self-reflexivity and, 52–59; sexuality in, 61–62; stylistic traits of, 57, 58; *The Tidewater Tales* and, 109–10; water-messages in, 89

McConnell, Frank, 68
Möbius strip, 52–53, 102, 132
Moby Dick, 115
Morrell, David, xiii, 13, 22, 68
The Muses of John Barth, xiii
Myth of the Birth of the Hero, 35

Mythotherapy, 15

The Odyssey, 61–62, 112
The 1001 Nights, 73, 119–20
Opera, 1

Passionate Virtuosity, xiii
Pennsylvania State University, 137
Poe, Edgar Allan, 104
A Portrait of the Artist as a Young Man, 51, 52, 57
Powell, Jerry, 77–78
Putnam's (publishers), 101

Raglan, Lord, 35, 73, 132
Rank, Otto, 35
Raper, Julius, 70
Reilly, Charlie, 83
Romer, Marjorie, 97

Sabbatical: male-female authorship and, 99, 101; publishing of, 101; realism mastery in, 108; reproductive metaphor in, 100; romanticism in, 105; self-reflexivity in, 105, 107–8; *The Tidewater Tale* and, 100–101, 110, 111–12, 116; title significance of, 106–7; twinning and, 101, 103, 105–6; Y symbol in, 101–2
Sartre, Jean Paul, 2, 14
Schickel, Richard, 4, 5
Schulz, Max, xiii, 69, 94, 102–3, 112, 116, 117
Scriptotherapy, 15, 16, 27
The Seventh Voyage, 120
Slethaug, Gordon, xiii, 107
Smith, Herbert, 17–18
Smith, John, 22
The Sot-Weed Factor: authorial power and, 70; Barth's objectives and, 21; bilateral philosophies in, 31; character development in, 29–30; comic aspects of, 23, 28–29; credibility of, 24–25, 29; *The End*

of the Road and, 26–27; *Giles Goat-Boy* and, 27; history of Maryland and, 21–24; literary criticism in, 27–28; literary imitation in, 25, 28, 30; metaphors in, 30–31; moral resolution and, 30; narrative variety in, 24; scriptotherapy in, 27; sexuality and, 30–31, 123; sexual rivalry in, 25–26; transformation creativity and, 32
The Sound and the Fury, 103
State University of New York, 35, 137
Stonehill, Brian, 94
Storytelling, art of, 67–68
Strehle, Susan, 86, 91
Strickland, Harriette Anne, 137
Swift, Jonathan, 47

Tharpe, Jac, xiii
The Tidewater Tales: bay analogy in, 109, 111; *Chimera* and, 112, 117; circularity and, 110; conclusion of, 117; coupling in, 110–11, 113–14, 116; environmental subplot of, 113; *LETTERS* and, 115; *Lost in the Funhouse* and, 109–10; male-female authorship and, 99; mythical references in, 112, 114; reproductive theme in, 100, 109, 112–13; *Sabbatical* and, 100–101, 110, 111–12, 116; self-reflexive analogies in, 109; supporting roles in, 114–15; as twin novel, 101, 103, 105; women's roles in, 114, 115
Tilton, John, 45
Tobin, Patricia, xiii, 75, 127
Tom Jones, 18, 24
Tristram Shandy, 2

Ulysses, 62, 103, 121
Understanding John Barth, xiii

Waldmeir, Joseph, xiii-xiv
Walkiewicz, E. P., xiii, 18, 92, 94
The Waste Land, 90, 92
Weixlmann, Joseph, xiv
Wolfe, Gregory, 128
Wroth, Lawrence, 22

Ziegler, Heide, xiii

About the Author

ZACK BOWEN is Professor and Chair of the Department of English at the University of Miami. He has published widely on modern literature, particularly on James Joyce and the Irish Renaissance. His books include *Padraic Colum* (1970), *Mary Lavin* (1975), *Musical Allusions in the Works of James Joyce* (1974), *A Companion to Joyce Studies* (co-edited with James Carens, Greenwood Press, 1984) and *Ulysses as a Comic Novel* (1990). He has served as editor or co-editor of *The Journal of Irish Literature* and *Irish Renaissance Annual*, and he is editor of a book publication series of critical essays in literature. He was associate editor of the *Dictionary of Irish Literature* (Greenwood Press, 1979) and the *Macmillan Dictionary of Irish Literature*, and he has produced, directed, or written commentary or notes for recordings of Joyce and Colum.

813.4
Bar

DATE DUE